SERIES EDITORS

Tracy L. Pellett **Jack Rutherford** **Claudia Blackman**

Skills, Drills & Strategies for
Basketball

Charlie Nix

Mississippi State University

Holcomb Hathaway, Publishers
Scottsdale, Arizona 85250

Library of Congress Cataloging-in-Publication Data

Nix, Charlie
    Skills, drills & strategies for basketball / Charlie Nix.
       p.   cm. — (The teach, coach, play series)
    Includes index.
    ISBN 1-890871-11-7
      1. Basketball. 2. Basketball—Training. I. Title: Skills, drills, and strategies for
basketball. II. Title: Basketball. III. Title. IV. Series.

GV885 .N59 2000

                                                99-053051

Holcomb Hathaway, Publishers
6207 North Cattle Track Road, Suite 5
Scottsdale, Arizona 85250
(480) 991-7881
www.hh-pub.com

10 9 8 7 6 5 4 3 2 1

ISBN 1-890871-11-7

Printed in the United States of America.

Contents

Preface

The books in the *Teach, Coach, Play* series emphasize a systematic learning approach to sports and activities. Both visual and verbal information are presented so that you can easily understand the material and improve your performance.

Built-in learning aids help you master each skill in a step-by-step manner. Using the cues, summaries, skills, drills, and illustrations will help you build a solid foundation for safe and effective participation now and in the future.

This text is designed to illustrate correct techniques and demonstrate how to achieve optimal results. Take a few minutes to become familiar with the textbook's organization and features. Knowing what to expect and where to look for material will help you get the most out of the textbook, your practice time, and this course.

TO THE INSTRUCTOR

Your needs are changing, your courses are changing, your students are changing, and the demands from your administration are changing. By setting out to create a series of books that addresses many of these changes, we've created a series that:

- Provides complete, consistent coverage of each sport—the basics through skills and drills to game strategies so you can meet the needs of majors and non-majors alike.
- Includes teaching materials so that new and recently assigned instructors have the resources they need to teach the course.
- Allows you to cover exactly the sports and activities you want with the depth of coverage you want.

What's in the *Teach, Coach, Play* Series?

- Nine activities:
    Skills, Drills, & Strategies for Badminton
    Skills, Drills, & Strategies for Basketball
    Skills, Drills, & Strategies for Bowling
    Skills, Drills, & Strategies for Golf

Skills, Drills, & Strategies for Racquetball
Skills, Drills, & Strategies for Strength Training
Skills, Drills, & Strategies for Swimming
Skills, Drills, & Strategies for Tennis
Skills, Drills, & Strategies for Volleyball
- Accompanying Instructor's Manuals

What's in the Student *Teach, Coach, Play* Textbooks?

The basic approach in all of the *Teach, Coach, Play* activity titles is to help students improve their skills and performance by building mastery from simple to complex levels.

The basic organization in each textbook is as follows:

Section 1 overviews history, organizations and publications, conditioning activities, safety, warm-up suggestions, and equipment.

Section 2 covers exercises or skills, participants, action involved, rules, facility or field, scoring, and etiquette.

Section 3 focuses on skills and drills or program design.

Section 4 addresses a broad range of strategies specifically designed to improve performance now and in the future.

Section 5 provides a convenient glossary of terms.

Supplements to Support You and Your Students

The *Teach, Coach, Play* books provide useful and practical instructional tools. Each activity is supported by its own manual. Each of these instructor's manuals includes classroom management notes, safety guidelines, teaching tips, ideas for inclusion of students with special needs, drills, lesson plans, evaluation notes, test bank, and a list of resources for you.

About the Author

Charlie Nix is an assistant professor of Health, Physical Education, Recreation, and Sport at Mississippi State University. He specializes in physical education teacher education (pedagogy) and statistics. Dr. Nix is an advocate of a physically active lifestyle and has nurtured a passion for basketball since junior high-school days. Nix coached both boy's and girl's high school and junior high school basketball teams for nine years in Kansas public schools, where he was known for his ability to teach fundamental skills, defense, and his love of the game to his athletes.

Dr. Nix was fortunate to coach and study basketball with two lengendary Kansas high school coaches: Tom Williams from Leoti and Duane Bissett from Holton. Since receiving his doctorate degree at the University of Alabama, Nix has been a professor at Northern Illinois University, Louisiana Tech University, and MSU. He has taught coaching of basketball and basketball activity courses during his higher education career.

Nix, his wife Suzanne, and their three children, Lon, Nolan, and Maggie, are avid basketball fans and attend every men's or women's collegiate game that comes to town.

This book is dedicated to the author's mother and father, Carol and Harding Nix, who taught him the importance of concentrating and "really" watching sport, while encouraging his constant pursuit of the ball.

Preliminaries

"The best athletes in the world play basketball."
"Basketball is the ultimate team sport."
*"Basketball combines high levels of skill with graceful movements
    and fast-paced action."*

These are typical descriptors applied to the sport of basketball. Although these phrases might generate considerable debate from other sport enthusiasts, basketball lovers clearly believe that theirs is the best and most challenging team sport in the world of sports today. Dr. James Naismith, the inventor of basketball, probably would agree, although his original intentions in designing the game didn't suggest that he was trying to develop the best team sport of our time.

HISTORY

As a physical education instructor in 1891, Dr. Naismith was asked by Dr. Luther S. Gulick, head of the physical education department at the International Young Men's Christian Association Training School in Springfield, Massachusetts, to design some indoor activity or physical training that would be of interest to students during the winter months. Football in the fall and baseball in the spring offered the students competitive games and activities they thoroughly enjoyed. During the winter "indoor" months, however, the activities consisted mostly of calisthenics, gymnastics, and marching, which did not have general appeal to the students. Thus, Naismith attempted to find a competitive game to be played indoors.

Naismith didn't invent basketball overnight. He tried indoor versions of other already defined sports such as rugby, soccer, and lacrosse. The indoor versions of these games proved to be too rough for gymnasium play. By trying these indoor sports first, though, Naismith was able to determine what would and wouldn't work well indoors. He wanted a game that didn't allow running with a ball or striking with an implement or propelling a ball into a goal. In the end, he decided to invent his own game.

So, in mid-December 1891, teaching a class of 18 men, Naismith debuted a game that used a soccer ball, which was to be placed with great accuracy into a high goal made from peach baskets. The rules at this time were not always clear, and Naismith didn't write them down until 1892. Originally, dribbling was excluded from the 13 rules. Naismith, however, incorporated dribbling into the game to prevent the players from throwing passes to themselves by bouncing the ball off the floor. Much like children's games today that establish rules as the game is being played, Naismith's new game began to evolve and change from the beginning.

Initially, Naismith didn't use the concept of the center jump ball to start the game, but he soon saw a need to include this modification after watching the rough free-for-all that took place with his original idea of both teams racing to mid-court to see who could get the ball first. The center jump rule was written into the rules by 1897. Several years later, in 1913, the concept of out-of-bounds play replaced the scramble to get a ball from the sidelines by whoever touches it first. Other modifications included the addition of free throws in 1894, making the double-dribble illegal in 1898, and the five-foul elimination rule in 1908.

Much of the popularity of basketball can be attributed to the process of institutionalization (Coakley, 1992). This includes the standardization of rules used throughout the YMCA organization, which enabled clubs and other organizations to sponsor teams and games. The first intercollegiate game was played in Minnesota. Yale instituted the first official schedule in 1896. That same year, the **American Athletic Union (AAU)** sponsored the first basketball tournament. The first professional league, the **National Basketball League,** was organized in 1898.

The AAU, and later the **National Collegiate Athletic Association (NCAA),** began to regulate the rules. By 1915, the role of officials, the size and weight of the ball, and the size and height of the basket were standardized.

The first book on basketball skills, *How to Play Basketball,* by George Hepbion, was published in 1904. At the time, coaches and players were developing and honing offensive and defensive strategies.

Finally, but not surprisingly, people started going to watch the games. Even in its first year, spectators were common at basketball games. Soon, playing arenas included seating for people who were interested in watching this new and wonderful indoor game.

Today the game continues to evolve and prosper. The **National Basketball Association (NBA)** is considered the most stable professional organization in sport. Basketball players are the most visible and highly marketed professional athletes. The Final Four weekend of the NCAA college basketball championships has become as exciting and anticipated as the Super Bowl in professional football or the World Series in Major League Baseball. Even at the high school and local level, basketball stirs the passion of its followers. More girls play interscholastic high school basketball than any other sport.

Perhaps the most phenomenal aspect of basketball's growth and popularity is its international scope. Almost 200 countries have basketball federations, and basketball has been part of the Olympic Games since 1936. The inclusion of NBA players in the Olympics beginning in 1992 enhanced the worldwide influence of basketball and secured its future in the world of sports.

The future of this sport continues to look promising. During off-season (the summer months), three-on-three tournaments are being conducted throughout cities in the United States and in more than 60 countries. Literally millions of people are playing this game either in organized competitions or through unorganized avenues. The game can be modified for two players to compete one-on-one or for two-on-two, three-on-three, four-on-four, and the full-court five-on-five variations. The game is played both indoors and outdoors.

At the organized level, the NBA continues to expand, with 29 cities currently represented. The **Continental Basketball Association (CBA)** has become a training or minor league for basketball. At least three other men's professional leagues exist in the United States at this time. As of late 1999, the **Women's National Basketball Association (WNBA)** has teams in 16 cities and is enjoying popularity with fans. Europe and Australia have professional leagues for men and women. Clearly, the future of basketball is bright. With its governing bodies willing to

American Athletic Union (AAU) *an organization established to regulate and supervise college athletics*

National Basketball League *the first professional league of basketball players, organized in 1898*

National Collegiate Athletic Association (NCAA) *established in 1910 as the new name for the American Athletic Union, organized to regulate and supervise college athletics*

National Basketball Association (NBA) *men's professional basketball organization*

Continental Basketball Association (CBA) *an organization that provides training and minor league experience*

Women's National Basketball Association (WNBA) *a professional basketball league for women run by the NBA*

make rule changes such as the 3-point shot in college and high school competition and the shot clock variations at different levels of play, basketball will continue to capture the interest of players and fans for years to come.

ORGANIZATIONS

The United States of America Basketball organization, USA Basketball, is the main organization responsible for men's and women's international competition. The organization is a leader in shaping the future of basketball in the United States and in international circles. For more information on USA Basketball, contact:

USA Basketball
5465 Mark Dabling Blvd.
Colorado Springs, CO 80918
Phone: (719) 590-4800
www.usabasketball.com

The governing body for international basketball competition is the Federation Internationale de Basketball (FIBA). For more information concerning international competition and rules, contact:

FIBA
PO Box 70 06 07
Kistlerhofstrasse 168
W-800 Munchen 70
Federal Republic of Germany
www.fiba.com

Within the United States, many governing bodies preside over several levels of organized basketball. For professional basketball, the National Basketball Association (NBA) provides leadership and support for its members, as well as helping to influence the marketing and sale of basketball paraphernalia worldwide. With its NBA licensing scheme of NBA logos, shirts, balls, and other items, the NBA generates more than $2 billion in sales per year to the general public. This helps keep the NBA and basketball in general in the public eye. For more information from the NBA, contact:

NBA
Attn: Rod Thorn, Assistant Director
Olympic Tower
645 Fifth Avenue
New York, NY 10022
www.nba.com
www.wnba.com

The National Collegiate Athletic Association (NCAA) controls competition for men and women at the collegiate levels of play for Divisions I, II, and III. The National Association for Intercollegiate Athletics (NAIA) provides the same type of leadership to its members at the collegiate level. The National Junior College Athletic Association (NJCAA) organizes competition for men and women at 2-year member institutions. For more information about collegiate men and women's basketball, contact:

NCAA
6201 College Boulevard
Overland Park, KS 66211-2424
Phone: (913) 339-1906
www.ncaa.org

NAIA
Two Warren Place, Suite 1450
6120 S. Yale Avenue
Tulsa, OK 74136-4223
Phone: (918) 494-8828
www.naia.org

NJCAA
PO Box 7305
Colorado Springs, CO 80933
Phone: (719) 590-9788
www.njcaa.org

The National Federation of State High School Associations (NFSHSA) represents most of the boys' and girls' basketball in high schools throughout the United States. The NFSHSA helps to provide leadership and rule changes for the 50 state high school associations. For more information on the NFHSSA, contact:

NFSHSA
11724 NW Plaza Circle
Box 20626
Kansas City, MO 64195
Phone: (816) 464-5400
www.nfshsa.org

The Amateur Athletic Union (AAU) has had an important impact on youth and adolescent boys' and girls' basketball in recent years. The AAU governs off-season and summer age-group competition, which has gained popularity across the United States. Tournaments are played primarily during the summer. Many junior high and high school kids have continued to hone their skills through the activities of this organization. For more information on the AAU, contact:

AAU National Office
3400 W. 86th Street
PO Box 68207
Indianapolis, IN 46268
Phone: (317) 872-2900

Finally, coaches' organizations have increased their influence on the sport of basketball. The National Association of Basketball Coaches of the United States (NABC) and the Women's Basketball Coaches Association (WBCA) have had significant roles as promoters of basketball coaches. These organizations help to guide discussion and address coaching issues, as well as promoting the coaching of basketball as a profession. For more information on these coaches associations, contact:

Women's Basketball Coaches
  Association
4646 B Lawrenceville Highway
Liburn, GA 30247
Phone: (770) 279-8027
www.wbca.org

National Association of
  Basketball Coaches
9300 W. 110th Street, Suite 640
Overland Park, KS 66210
Phone: (913) 469-1001

PUBLICATIONS

Literally hundreds of books have been written about basketball. A few examples are:

Wooden, John R. (1999). *Practical Modern Basketball* (Coaching Legends in Basketball), 3rd Ed. Allyn & Bacon.

Carril, Pete, Dan White, and Bobby Knight (1997). *The Smart Take from the Strong: The Basketball Philosophy of Pete Carril.* Simon & Schuster.

Kresse, John and Richard Jablonski (1998). *The Complete Book of Man to Man Offense* (The Art &Science of Coaching Series). John Kreese Sports Publishing.

These books can be found in libraries and purchased in bookstores, sporting goods stores, and other locations where sports publications are sold. In addition, journals and magazines about basketball are published. Some of these highlight past accomplishments and include statistics and summaries of previous basketball seasons. Others discuss upcoming seasons, predicting the order of finish in the NBA or college conferences. These typically highlight the expected roster make-up of teams and discuss pluses and minuses of the upcoming season based on performances of the previous season. They also include schedules for your favorite teams. *Street and Smith, Athos, The Sporting News,* and *Dick Vitale's Basketball* examine the collegiate and pro games in this way. *Coaching Women's Basketball* is the official membership publication of the WBCA.

CONDITIONING

Some of the best athletes in the world play basketball. Basketball players must possess many physical attributes to be able to perform at a highly skilled level: physical strength, endurance, durability, flexibility, agility, quickness, eye-hand coordination, rhythm, and balance. These traits can be improved through an appropriate conditioning program. Also, basketball players must train the mental as well as the physical domain. The mind/body relationship is the foundation of total conditioning.

Principles of Conditioning

When developing an overall conditioning program for basketball players, the following principles of conditioning should be considered.

Principle of Overload. The **overload principle** holds that the intensity of a workout must be greater than normal routine in relation to a person's existing state of fitness. In general, overloading means doing more, faster, higher, more often.

Principle of Progression. As physical capacity improves, the duration, intensity, and frequency of workouts should be manipulated and increased to assure gains in fitness.

Principle of Specificity. Results of conditioning are specific to the activities performed. Therefore, one must practice a skill to perform that skill. For the basketball player, the skills important to basketball should be studied and practiced.

Principle of Individuality. Each individual has a unique response to each specific exercise. Therefore, conditioning programs for basketball players should consider the physical and psychological uniqueness of each individual.

Principle of Maintenance. Use it or lose it. Once a basketball player gains a desired level of conditioning, he or she must work continually to maintain the existing state of fitness.

General Conditioning

Conditioning for basketball initially should emphasize these major fitness areas: Muscular strength, muscular endurance, cardiovascular endurance, and flexibility.

Progressive Resistance Program

Weight training, following a progressive resistance program, is probably the best way for the basketball player to develop **muscular strength** and **endurance.**

A progressive resistance weight training program utilizes free weights (barbells and weights) and weight machines such as Cybex or Nautilus equipment.

principle of overload
doing more than normal to improve fitness

principle of progression
a gradual increase in the amount of exercise done over a period of time

principle of specificity
specific kinds of activity to build specific components of physical fitness

principle of individuality
each individual's unique response to different activities

principle of maintenance
retaining the present level of fitness once the desired level is reached

muscular strength
ability of a muscle or muscle group to exert maximum force one time

muscular endurance
ability of a muscle or muscle group to repeat a movement again and again for an extended time

The basketball player concentrates on working all major muscle groups to prepare the body for maximum performance (principle of specificity). This includes muscle groups in the arm-shoulder area, back and abdomen, pelvis and hips, and leg muscle groups.

In general, this training includes six to eight repetitions (reps) of a given exercise in one to three sets at least three times per week. Following the principle of overload, the player works at 50%–80% of maximum effort per exercise depending on whether strength or endurance is the primary focus. If strength gain is important, the player might do six to eight reps in sets of one to three, working at 70%–80% of maximum effort. If endurance is to be improved, the workouts might consist of 12 to 15 reps (up to 20–25 reps) of one to three sets at 50%–60% of maximum effort.

The principle of progression also is applied to weight training. One or two repetitions are added each week to each exercise. Usually one repetition is added to arm and upper body exercises and two repetitions to leg and lower-body exercises. In addition, as the repetitions reach 10–12 for each strength exercise, weight (5 to 10 pounds) is added to each exercise, with six to eight repetitions.

Another way to apply the principle of progression is to increase the number of sets for each exercise. For the beginner or untrained player, one set will do for the first 12–14 weeks. Eventually, to gain more strength or endurance, an additional set (up to three sets) is performed per exercise.*

Aerobic Training

aerobic training or endurance ability of the cardiovascular system to function efficiently at a high rate for an extended time using oxygen as the main source of energy

cardiovascular endurance ability to perform physical activities for extended periods using the heart, lung, and vascular system

Aerobic training involves the player's cardiovascular system. **Cardiovascular endurance** is the body's ability to use the heart, lung, and vascular (blood) system to do work over an extended time. Usually, continuous exercise for 20–30 minutes is required to improve the cardiovascular system.

This continuous exercise is known as *aerobic exercise* because the body has to use oxygen as the main source of energy. Aerobic means *with oxygen*. Generally, for the basketball player, running-type exercises are emphasized for aerobic workouts. This is logical because the basketball player must run almost continuously in today's fast-paced game.

To determine exercise intensity or how hard the player should run to improve his/her cardiovascular (aerobic) endurance, *maximum aerobic capacity* should be considered. Everyone has a certain limit to which his/her heart and circulation system is able to provide oxygen to the working muscle tissues (principle of individuality). Therefore, although each individual's maximum aerobic capacity is different, most healthy players can use the method to determine individual exercise intensity.

In determining individual exercise intensity, one calculates his/her maximum heart rate and then tries to exercise at between 60% and 80% of this maximum. Maximum heart rate can be estimated by subtracting one's age from 220, then taking this number to calculate exercise intensity at 60% to 80% of maximum.

For example, a 22-year-old should exercise at heart rate levels between 120 and 160 beats per minute. If the player's heart rate does not reach this threshold (120–160 beats per minute), more intensity is needed to improve cardiovascular functioning. If the same player's heart rate exceeds 160 beats per minute, the player might want to decrease the intensity of the workout.

---

*It is not the intent of this book to give a complete or comprehensive discussion of weight training. For more information and other suggestions for muscular strength and endurance improvement, consult your local library or health club for books dealing specifically with weight training techniques.

The main type of workout for improving cardiovascular endurance involves continuous slow running for at least 30 minutes, three or four times per week—in essence, running long distances at slow speeds. Also, repetition running is beneficial in aerobic training. This involves repetitions of comparatively long distances (800 meters) with relatively complete recovery, usually by walking after each effort.

Workouts that include swimming or cycling also may be used to build cardiovascular endurance. These workouts must entail 30 minutes of continuous exercise. Using more than one method of aerobic training, called *cross-training,* might help the player avoid injuries to joints and muscles caused by repeated repetition of the same workouts.

Anaerobic Training

Anaerobic training or **endurance,** sometimes called speed endurance, helps the player develop the capacity to withstand fatigue. This is essential in the game of basketball.

For anaerobic training or endurance, the basketball player should do activities that can be done in fast intervals. This might include running consecutive sprints of 200 meters or less. Also, running up and down stadium or gymnasium steps, hill running, and **Fartlek training** can improve anaerobic power. Fartlek training can advance both aerobic and anaerobic fitness. This is a form of training featuring informal fast-slow running and usually involves running over natural surfaces such as grass or golf courses, with emphasis on fast (anaerobic) running. Other types of running, such as sprinting, walking, and continuous fast-running, are commonly combined for distances up to three or four miles.

> **anaerobic training or endurance** short duration, explosive activities for which more oxygen is required than is being supplied
>
> **Fartlek training** a technique involving running on varied terrain at varying speeds

Flexibility Conditioning

Finally, **flexibility** training should be incorporated in all conditioning sessions. Lack of flexibility is believed to be one of the most frequent causes of improper or poor movement and also may contribute to many athletic injuries (Swanbom, 1980). Poor flexibility requires the muscles to work harder, which results in loss of energy. Increasing flexibility of the ankles, legs, hips, and trunk helps to conserve energy and allows for greater muscle efficiency, which helps the basketball player run faster and jump higher (Swanbom, 1980).

Flexibility is developed by stretching the range of motion through which the joint moves. Attempting to progressively increase the range of motion through which one attempts to move applies the overload principle. Development of the basketball player's flexibility must be a part of every conditioning program. Thus, flexibility exercises are included in all off-season, preseason, and competitive season workouts.

The two major kinds of stretching or flexibility exercises are static and ballistic. **Static stretching** is a slow, gradual, passive stretch in which the muscles and joints are held in the position of greatest possible length (Devries, 1962). **Ballistic stretching** is a bouncing, jerking motion in which body segments are stretched with these jerks or pulls. Static stretching usually is recommended because there is less chance of stretching too far and thereby causing tissue damage. Also, static stretching requires less energy and has been shown to reduce post-exercise muscle distress (Devries, 1962).

Flexibility exercises are included in every workout. Also, flexibility exercises are done prior to basketball practice, games, and other workout activities to warm up the muscles and joints. In accordance with the principle of individuality, the body should not be forced or pushed beyond individual limits.

> **flexibility** ability to move freely through a full, nonrestricted, painfree range of motion
>
> **static stretching** stretching a muscle slowly and passively, then holding it in position for an extended time
>
> **ballistic stretching** repetitive, bouncing movements used to stretch a specific muscle

Finally, flexibility exercises are done after practice, games, and other conditioning workouts. The following flexibility exercises are especially important for the basketball player.

■ Exercise 1: Head and Neck

Standing with feet in parallel position, the back straight and the shoulders pulled down and back:

1. Begin with head on right shoulder.
2. Roll head forward to left shoulder (2 counts). Roll back to right shoulder (2 counts).
3. Roll head one and one-half times (circle and one-half) around so it ends up on left shoulder (4 counts).
4. Repeat entire sequence starting with left shoulder. One complete sequence consists of both right and left. Repeat each complete sequence four times.
5. Keep shoulders down to increase possible range of motion of neck.

■ Exercise 2: Upper Extremities and Hamstrings

hamstring *one of the tendons at the back of the knee*

This exercise involves the muscles of the arms and shoulders, as well as **hamstrings** and ankles. Standing with feet in parallel position, the back straight and the shoulders pulled down and back:

1. Reach right arm straight up, elevating the right shoulder. (2 counts)
2. Reach left arm straight up, elevating left shoulder. (2 counts)
   Repeat each side four times. (16 counts total)
3. Reach both arms straight overhead and bend over. (8 counts)
4. Hang in this position. (8 counts)
5. While gently holding onto ankles, bend knees slowly. (4 counts)
6. Straighten knees slowly. (4 counts)
7. Repeat the bending and straightening three times. As you straighten knees, try to decrease angle between rib cage and thighs (quadriceps) . Roll up in 8 counts to starting position.
8. Repeat entire sequence three times. Each sequence consists of 64 counts.

■ Exercise 3: Upper Torso, Shoulder, and Pectoral

pectoral *chest area*

To develop the upper torso, shoulder, and **pectoral** muscles, stand with the feet in parallel position, the back straight, arms down to side and shoulders pulled down and back, then:

1. Circle right arm straight upward as near to ear as possible, pushing arm farther back on counts one, two, three, and four.
2. On counts five and six, circle arm one full circle backward.
3. After completing the circle, be sure arm is straight up in the air next to ear on count seven. It stops in this position and returns to starting position on count eight.
4. Repeat the same sequence with left arm.
5. Do the same sequence with both arms.
6. Repeat entire sequence (right arm, left arm, both arms) three times. Each sequence consists of 24 counts.
7. On the third sequence, elevate onto your toes and balance as you complete the exercise.

■ Exercise 4: Abductors (Groin), Hamstrings, and Lower Back

To exercise the **abductor** (groin) muscles, hamstrings, and lower back, sit on the floor and open the legs as far as possible, keeping the feet in dorsiflex (toes pulled back) and the back straight, then:

1. Gently bring torso forward, trying to keep your back straight. Hold this position for a count of 48. As the range of motion increases, gravity will assist the effectiveness of this exercise.

2. Using an eight-count transition, return to starting position, rotate torso to the right, and go over right leg. Try to line up spine with right leg. While keeping the back straight, try to decrease the angle between ribs and thigh. Hold this position for a count of 48.

3. Using an eight-count transition, return to starting position, rotate torso to left, and go over left leg. Hold this position for a count of 48.

4. Using an eight-count transition, return to starting position and repeat the first sequence, going straight forward. Hold this position for 48 counts. You should notice a slight increase in range of motion when you repeat the forward sequence.

abductors *muscles that move away from axis or trunk*

■ Exercise 5: Adductor (Groin)

To exercise the **adductor** muscles in the groin:

1. Sitting on the floor, pull both feet in and lift up on heels.

2. As you lift on the ankles, push your elbows into inner thighs, forcing knees down.

3. Push lower back toward pelvis. Back should remain as straight as possible, with shoulders pulled down and back.

4. Once the above static position has been reached, hold for 64 counts. Back must remain straight and pressure should be applied to inner thighs to increase range of motion in groin area.

adductor *muscles that draw a part toward the median line of the body or toward the axis of an extremity*

■ Exercise 6: Tensor Fasciae Latae, Gluteal, and Spine

This exercise develops the **tensor fasciae, gluteal,** and spine muscles. Start by sitting on the floor, then:

1. Cross right leg over straight left leg, holding onto right knee with left arm and pulling it as close to the chest as possible.

2. Place right hand on the ground behind right buttocks and use it to assist in keeping the back straight. Rotate upper torso toward the right as you gently resist, holding onto right knee with left arm. Hold this position for 48 counts.

3. Reverse position of body and do other side. Again, hold position for 48 counts.

tensor fasciae latae *small muscle at the front and side of the hip*

gluteal *related to gluteus muscles, the large muscles of the buttocks*

■ Exercise 7: Quadriceps

This exercise focuses on the **quadriceps** muscle.

1. Lying on left side of body, extend bent right leg as far behind as possible. The leg must stay bent and pushed as far as possible behind body. Holding onto right leg with right arm will assist in pushing leg behind torso. The body must remain straight, providing resistance to the stretching quadriceps. Hold this position for 48 counts.

2. Repeat exercise with left leg. Hold this position for 48 counts.

quadriceps *the great extensor muscle at front of thigh*

acetabulum *cup-shaped socket in hip bone*

spinal rotation *rotary movement of spine in horizontal plane*

■ Exercise 8: Acetabulum, Spinal Rotation, Hamstring, and Ankle

This exercise works the **acetabulum** by **spinal rotation,** as well as the hamstring and ankle.

1. Lying flat on your back, pull right knee in toward right armpit and hold in this position for 16 counts.
2. Holding onto knee, rotate (circle) leg, which will loosen and lubricate the joint.
3. With knee bent, place right foot on side of knee, keeping left leg straight, and pull knee to floor with left hand. Rotate body to opposite of right knee, and reach to the right with a straight arm, focusing on right hand with your eyes. This will create a spiral rotation of the spine. Hold this position for 48 counts.
4. Straighten leg gradually, pulling it toward chest. Leg straightens in 8 counts.
5. Flex (pull toes back) ankle and point (point toes down) ankle 8 times each. Total counts for flexion equal 16.
6. Rotate (circle) the ankle 8 times to the right and repeat 8 times to the left. Each rotation takes 2 counts to complete for a total of 32 counts.
7. Gradually move leg to the side and return it to starting position.
8. Repeat entire sequence with left leg.

■ Exercise 9: Upper Torso Isolation

1. From a standing position with both arms extended straight to the side, move entire torso atop a fixed pelvis toward the right. Reach toward the right as far as possible without disturbing lower body. (2 counts)
2. Repeat #1, reaching toward the left. (2 counts)
3. Alternate from side to side 12 times each. Total counts equal 48.

General conditioning also should include workouts with the basketball. Basketball players can refine their skills and at the same time condition themselves both physically and mentally. Shooting skills should be the primary emphasis, and if shooting workouts are repetitive, both anaerobic power and muscular endurance can be improved through these activities.

Specific Conditioning

While general conditioning allows the basketball player time to improve or develop overall fitness and skills, specific training prepares the body physically and mentally for the rigors of playing the game of basketball. The athlete needs to have a period to develop the high levels of fitness and muscle conditioning necessary for competition. This conditioning is much more intense than the general program. In addition to flexibility, cardiovascular endurance and anaerobic power, and muscular strength and endurance, quickness and agility drills are added.

agility *ability to change or alter, quickly and accurately, the direction of body movement*

circuit training *a series of exercise stations for strength training, flexibility, and endurance*

Agility is essential to basketball (Strand, Scantling, & Johnson, 1997). It is a game of constant motion and changes of direction in the flow of the game. To reach their potential and to be competitive, players must be as quick and agile as their body limits will allow. Fartlek training and repetition running can help improve quickness, because these methods develop anaerobic power. In addition, specific agility drills can be introduced to improve agility and quickness and to meet the principle of specificity requirements.

For endurance training, at least two new methods might be introduced. **Circuit training** uses weights and machines to do endurance exercises, but the amount of weight used to perform each activity is usually one-half of one's maximal effort and each exercise is done for a specified period (usually 30 seconds to one minute). The objective is to see how many repetitions can be performed within this timeframe.

Plyometrics is used to enhance jumping ability and improve leg strength and endurance. The box heights may vary, and repetitive jumping is the key. Plyometrics can be included as part of a circuit.

Finally, defensive drills, ball-handling skills, and rebounding drills may be combined with the shooting drills from the general conditioning program to continue skill development. The following specific conditioning program provides an example for the basketball player and coach/teacher to consider.

plyometrics jumping from an elevated surface (box) onto the floor and then rebounding (jumping) back into the air as high as possible

Basketball-Specific Conditioning Program

I. Warm-up

A. Light jogging—1/2 mile. Run with short, easy stride, carrying arms low and relaxed. Run all the way without stopping.

B. Exercises
  1. Fingertip pushups (10–15).
  2. Leg spreads (20).
  3. Crunches—hands crossed over shoulders (25).
  4. Flexibility exercises (performed before and after any workout).
     a. Pre-workout stretches
        1. Exercise 1 Head and Neck
        2. Exercise 2 Upper Extremities and Hamstring
        3. Exercise 3 Upper Torso, Shoulder, and Pectoral
        4. Exercise 4 Abductors (Groin), Hamstring, and Lower Back
        5. Exercise 5 Adductor (Groin)
        6. Exercise 6 Tensor Fasciae Latae, Gluteal, and Spine
        7. Exercise 7 Quadriceps
        8. Exercise 8 Acetabulum, Spine Rotation, Hamstring, and Ankle
     b. Post-workout stretches
        1. Exercise 2 Repeat
        2. Exercise 9 Upper Torso Isolation
        3. Exercise 4 Repeat
        4. Exercise 5 Repeat
        5. Exercise 7 Repeat

II. Endurance

A. Run stadium or gymnasium steps 25 times up and down.

B. Circuit training—six stations
  1. Dips: Do as many as you can in one minute.
  2. Leg raises: Do as many reps as you can in one minute.
  3. Toe raises: Do as many reps as you can in one minute.
  4. Squat thrusts: Do as many as you can in one minute.
  5. Curls: Do as many reps as you can in one minute.
  6. Box hopping (plyometrics): Keep doing for one minute.

The loads should be about one-half of the player's maximal effort. He/she is given a trial to see how long it takes him/her to complete this series of exercises, and then is assigned a "target time" approximately one-third faster than his/her recorded time. As soon as he/she can complete the circuit in this time, the loads are increased, he/she is again timed, and a new target time is established.

III. Quickness and agility

A. Acceleration sprinting: Jog 50 meters, stride 50 meters, sprint 100 meters, and walk 100 meters. Repeat four times.

B. Repetition running: 10 to 15 consecutive 200 meter sprints with 90 seconds rest between each sprint (strive for 30 seconds/spring; follow M, W, F schedule).

C. On alternate days (Tues., Thurs.) use Fartlek training—three miles.

D. Every day use the following two agility drills (5 minutes):

1. Run through your defensive steps as quickly as possible—go right, left, forward, and back

2. Quick step—see how many times your right foot hits the ground in one minute. Try to increase the number of times it hits each day.

IV. Work on skills—every other day

A. Ball handling

1. Fingertip drills

a. Continuously tap ball between both hands using fingertips, with arms raised above the head.

b. Use same tapping action with arms held straight in front of body.

2. Pass ball around your mid-section.

3. Single-leg circle—both legs: Pass ball from hand to hand around one leg; switch to other leg; pass around both legs.

4. Figure 8 both ways: Pass ball from hand to hand in a figure 8 pattern around and between each leg.

5. Spin ball on finger.

6. Dribble ball on side using fingertips on one side of the body in a stationary position. To switch hands, practice a behind-the-back and/or between-the-leg dribble.

7. Dribble around and through legs.

8. Dribble two balls in and out of rhythm.

9. Throw ball up in air. Slap front of legs and catch ball behind back (work up from one).

10. Ball handling on the move

a. Low dribble (closely guarded)

b. High dribble (for speed)

c. Stop and go (change of pace)

d. Switch dribble (keep it low)

e. Reverse

f. Fake reverse

g. Combinations

B. Foul shooting (10 minutes): Shoot two free throws, dribble hard down court, pull up and shoot a jump shot, then shoot two free throws, repeat.

C. Tap drills (6 minutes)

1. Get low in a good defensive stance. Go up and down the court working on the advance step, retreat step, and swing step. Don't go too fast, but instead make sure you are working hard and executing each step properly.

2. Standard tap drill with the ball: Put it on the board six times and then in the basket. Work on both hands.

D. Defensive drill (4 minutes)

1. Get low in a good defensive stance. Go up and down the court working on the advance step, retreat step, and swing step. Don't go too fast, but instead make sure you are working hard and executing each step properly.

E. Jump rope (5 minutes)

F. Scrimmage full court

A third phase of conditioning for the basketball player should be done on the court and be included as part of any team or group practice session. Many drills that have competitive skill elements can also be used to maintain fitness levels already gained (principle of maintenance). Motivation is a key component of conditioning. By including conditioning in the practice session and using drills that augment overall play, players will be able to enhance and maintain the fitness levels they have already achieved.

An infinite number of drills can be beneficial. The following is a sample of drills for maintenance of the conditioning program:

1. Full-court conditioning drill. This is done without the use of a basketball. Have two equal lines, one on the right side of the basket and the other on the left. The first player in line turns and faces the second; he/she becomes the defensive player. He/she places his/her hands behind his/her back, locking his/her thumbs. Upon command, the players start to run from one end of the court to the other. At the other end, they switch assignments.

2. Stop and go. The players form five lines at the end line. On the whistle, they run as fast and as far as they can until the next whistle. This means "stop in your tracks." Each succeeding whistle means go, stop, go, etc. This drill sharpens reflexes and makes the players run at top speed.

3. Dribbling conditioning drills. The team is divided into two lines at the end of the court. At the command, the player dribbles down the court with his/her right hand and returns dribbling with his/her left hand.

4. Four-corner drill. The team sets up in equal lines at the four corners of the gym. Starting with one ball, the first player hands off to the second player and breaks directly toward the second line (counter-clockwise). The player with the ball hits him/her with a baseball pass on the inside of the court. The receiver then throws a chest pass to the first player in the second line, who hands off to the next player and takes off, looking for a baseball pass. This is repeated until everyone has had a turn.

5. Shuttle relay. Each player runs to a line at forecourt, back to the starting line, then to the mid-court line, back to the starting line, then to a three-quarter line, back to the starting line, to the end line, and back to the starting line.

6. Floor-length half-court sprints. Three players spread out across the end line. On the signal, they sprint to the half-court line (center line) and then ease up and cross the opposite end line. They line up to return as soon as the last threesomes have crossed the end line.

7. 3-player weave—full court. The middle player rebounds the ball and passes to one of the wings, goes behind him/her, and cuts back to receive a pass from the player coming from the other side. They proceed down the floor, always cutting behind the player to whom they pass and then cutting back to receive a pass from the third player.

WARM-UP

Pre-game warm-up and pre-practice warm-up are important as preparation for an extremely vigorous activity such as basketball. The body has to be prepared properly for the vast demands that will be placed upon it during a game or practice.

The warm-up should begin with light jogging and movements that will raise the heart rate and "awaken" the body for further exertion and expenditure of energy. Basketball players might jog around the court during pre-game activities, or they might do control, speed, and off-hand dribbling the length of the court before practice. Defensive slides also can be used.

Flexibility exercises should follow, to get the joints and muscles ready to move easily through their full range of motion. Static stretches should be performed initially as they use less energy and help prevent injury to joints and tissue. Previously, nine flexibility exercises were introduced. These exercises should be included in every pre-game or pre-practice warm-up:

Exercise 1 Head and neck

Exercise 2 Upper extremities and hamstring

Exercise 3 Upper torso, shoulder, and pectoral

Exercise 4 Abductors (groin), hamstring, and lower back

Exercise 5 Abductor (groin)

Exercise 6 Tensor fasciae latae, gluteal, and spine

Exercise 7 Quadriceps

Exercise 8 Acetabulum, spinal rotation, hamstring, and ankle

Exercise 9 Isolates the upper torso (an excellent post-game or post-practice stretch to facilitate the proper warm-down following strenuous activity)

Ball-handling activities should follow the flexibility exercises. These are done to help the basketball player get the "feel of the ball" and to continue a gradual build-up of physical activity. The following skills are recommended:

1. Fingertip drills. "Pass" the ball back and forth between the fingertips of both hands. The arms initially are raised above the head. After about 20–30 seconds, lower them until they are straight out from the shoulder in front of the body. Follow with another 20–30 seconds of fingertip passing.

2. Pass ball around mid-section of the body. Pass the ball around the trunk of the body for 20–30 seconds as rapidly as possible. Then change the direction of the pass for an additional 20–30 seconds.

3. Pass ball around both legs. Follow the same procedure as described in item 2.

4. Single leg circles. Pass the ball around one leg and reverse direction for 20–30 second bouts. Use both legs.

5. Figure 8 both ways. Spread the legs wider than shoulder-width and begin passing the ball in a figure 8 pattern around, behind, and in front of each leg. Do this for 20–30 seconds, then reverse the direction for an additional 20–30 seconds.

6. Drop catches. In a crouched position, pass (drop) the ball between the legs, catch it behind the legs, then in front of the legs, etc., as it passes between the legs. This also can be done by dropping the ball between the legs and then catching it with the left hand in front of the legs and the right hand in back of the legs. Then, on successive "drops," reverse the hands (right in front, left in back, etc.) for 20–30 seconds.

7. Dribble around and through legs. Use a fast, low dribble to move the ball around, between, and through the legs. Fingertip control of the ball is important.

Following the flexibility and ball-handling exercises, most teams continue the warm-up using the fundamental skills of basketball—passing drills, shooting drills, rebounding drills, and combination drills. These drills increase the activity and energy expenditure and also prepare the players mentally by using gamelike patterns or movements. The drills chosen for pre-game warm-ups vary from team to team and are familiar to the player. These drills are used in practice; therefore, players can easily execute them and can concentrate on mentally preparing for the game.

Coaches and teachers want their players to get their heart rate elevated and to "break a sweat" during warm-ups. Also, coaches and teachers want their players to have many opportunities to practice shooting, especially if they are the visiting team and are not accustomed to the setting. No precise routine is stipulated. The following routines are merely suggestions. It does help the players to practice the routine and to use the same routine before each game.

PRE-GAME WARM-UP ROUTINE

1. Light jogging—defensive slides (1 to 2 minutes)
2. Flexibility exercises (previously discussed)
3. Ball-handling exercises (previously discussed)
4. All-pass drill—See Drill 1 in Section 3
   Use chest pass, one-hand push pass, bounce pass, two-handed overhand pass
5. 3-line, half-court lay-up drill (below)
6. 2-line dribble lay-up or jump shot drill (below)
7. Spot shooting (below)
8. Tipping drill (below)
9. 5-man weave half court (below)

Pre-Game Routine #5

Three-Line, Half-Court Lay-up Drill

Use three lines of players starting at half-court, with the wide players cheating down one stride for timing purposes (see Figure 1.1). The middle player (1) starts the drill by passing to 3 and then following behind 3. Then 2 moves in to meet the pass from 3, 3 makes a pass to 2 and follows behind for rebound position (see Figure 1.2). Then 1 gets in position to receive a pass from 2 and 2 passes to 1 for a layup; 2 continues to free throw line extended to receive outlet pass from 3; 1 continues wide and starts a return to the end of the line; 3 makes overhead outlet pass to 2 and follows his/her pass; 1 goes to the end of the line; 3 is wide and continues to the end of the line; 2 passes the ball to the next middle player and stays wide to return to the end of the line. For continuation of the drill, middle player starts ball in opposite direction from which he/she received it. When players become familiar with responsibilities, use two balls.

Figure 1.1 (on left)
3-line half-court lay-up drill.

Figure 1.2 (on right)
Position for rebound.

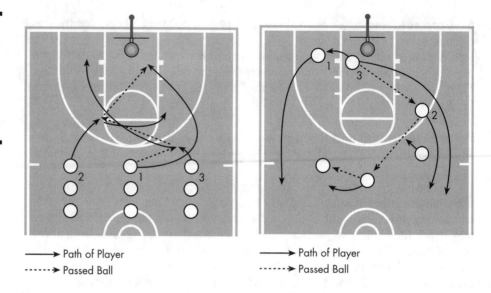

———➤ Path of Player
------➤ Passed Ball

———➤ Path of Player
------➤ Passed Ball

Pre-Game Routine #6

Two-Line Dribble Lay-up or Jump Shot Drill

The players are either in a rebound line (O's) or the shooting line (X's) (see Figure 1.3). The first player in the shooting line dribble-drives hard to the basket and shoots a lay-up or pulls up for the jump shot. The first player in the rebound line retrieves the shot, passes the ball to the next player in the shooting line, and goes to the end of the line. The shooter goes to the end of the rebound line. Two or three balls may be used, and the shooting line is moved to the other side (left) of the court after each player shoots several times from the right side.

Pre-Game Routine #7

Spot Shooting

Players individually shoot from areas where they expect to get a shot in a game situation. Each player should get 20–25 shots to adjust to the surrounding conditions. Some coaches like to have half the squad spot-shoot while the other half does flexibility exercises, ball-handling exercises, or passing drills; then they switch.

Pre-Game Routine #8

Tipping Drill

The players line up in one line (see Figure 1.4). The first player (X1) tosses the ball off the backboard and tips the rebound back against the board. X1 quickly moves and X2 tips the next rebound up against the board. This is repeated until each player makes a tip. If a player is small and cannot jump high enough for a tip back, he/she should jump-catch the ball and push the ball back up to the board before the feet hit the floor.

Figure 1.3
Two-line dribble lay-up or jump shot drill.

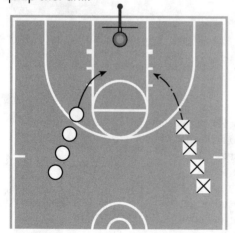

———➤ Path of Player
—·—➤ Dribbled Ball

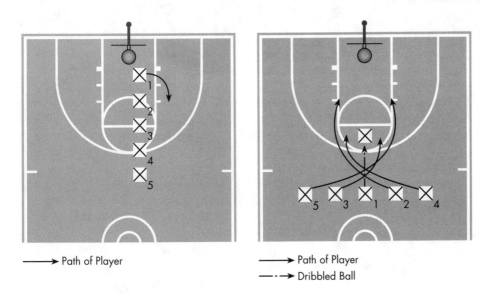

⟶ Path of Player

⟶ Path of Player
— · ⟶ Dribbled Ball

Pre-Game Routine # 9

5-Man Weave Half Court

This is done as described in Drill 9 on page 37, but a lay-up is added at the end. One player takes the ball and dribbles to the free throw line and pivots so his/her back is to the basket. The four remaining players continue their weave and begin to cut down the lane toward the basket; the pivot player passes to a cutter, who drives for a lay-up (see Figure 1.5).

The Game

The game of basketball is often considered the most athletic and fast-paced game in today's sporting world. Its popularity continues to rise among participants and spectators alike. This popularity can be attributed in part to the fact that an entire spectrum of people play basketball. Boys and girls play in youth-sponsored programs and on junior high/middle school and high school teams. Men and women play on college teams as well as professional leagues throughout the United States and the world. Wheelchair basketball has become one of the most popular sports for physically challenged players. Players continue to participate in 40- and 50-year-old and older recreational leagues around the nation.

In short, basketball is a game played by two teams of five players each, in which one team attempts to advance a ball into its front court by passing, dribbling, or handing it among the team members in an effort to make a basket over the other team's defense. Upon scoring a basket or losing the ball to the other team, the former team retreats into its back court and attempts to prevent the opponent from scoring.

The nature of the game and its rules vary with respect to age, skill level, and competitive goals. In this book we focus on men's and women's collegiate rules and game descriptives.

FUNDAMENTAL SKILLS

The fundamental skills for college-level basketball will be discussed in detail in Section 3. Specifically, the offensive ball-handling skills of passing, receiving, dribbling, pivoting, faking, and shooting must be mastered for the best competitive results. The following types of passes are basic to fundamental basketball:

- **Chest pass**
- **One-handed push pass**
- **Bounce pass**
- **Two-handed overhead pass**
- **Flip pass**
- **Baseball pass**

chest pass a two-handed pass pushed from the front of the passer's chest toward the receiver's chest on a horizontal plane

one-handed push pass a pass made with one hand, initiated from the side of the body, about shoulder height

19

bounce pass *a pass that strikes the floor once before it reaches the receiver*

two-handed overhead pass *a pass made with two hands, initiated high over the head*

flip pass *a pass made with one hand when exchanging the ball at close range*

baseball pass *a long down-court pass thrown with an overhand throwing motion*

jump shot *a shot taken after the shooter has jumped into the air*

free throw shot *an unguarded shot from the free-throw line that results from a foul by an opponent*

lay-up shot *a shot taken close to the basket, usually with one hand*

transition skills *skills that allow one team to rapidly change from offense to defense and vice versa.*

offensive rebounding *rebounding the ball at the offensive end of the floor when your team is the offensive team*

defensive rebounding *rebounding the ball at the opponent's end of the court when your team is the defensive team*

fast break *a situation in which the defensive team gains possession of the ball and moves into scoring position so quickly that its players outnumber the opponents downcourt*

defense *the team without the ball, whose objective is to keep the opponent from scoring*

offense *the team that has possession of the ball; also refers to the method a team uses to score baskets, as well as a team's scoring ability*

man-to-man defense *a team defense in which each defensive player is assigned to guard a specific opponent*

Dribbling skills include the controlled, speed, cross-over, and behind-the-back dribble. Pivoting, faking, and body-balance skills enable a player to master body-control fundamentals. Finally, the **jump shot, free-throw shot,** and **lay-up shot** are basic to offensive shooting fundamentals.

A second category of fundamental skills is the **transition skills.** **Offensive rebounding** and **defensive rebounding** often start the transition from one end of the court to the other. The **fast break** is an important component in the transition game, from both an offensive and a defensive perspective.

The final fundamental skills comprise the defensive group. These skills prevent or hinder an opponent's ability to score. Players and teams have to learn how to defend the ball handler plus a player without the ball and know what to do when outnumbered by the other team. The basics of **defense** start with the proper stance, positioning and footwork.

Team **offense** blends the five players to utilize fundamental skills that will accomplish team outcomes. Team offense is predicated on preferred style of play, type of players who comprise the team, and opponent strengths and weaknesses.

Offenses are designed to compete against the basic defenses that the other team might utilize. The main defenses are man-to-man and zone. **Man-to-man defense** refers to each player guarding or being responsible for an opponent in a one-on-one situation. A **zone defense** refers to players guarding any opposing player who might enter a specified area that each defender is responsible to protect. Zones are named for the formation of the players used to protect given areas. Common zones are the 2–3, 1–3–1, 3–2, and 2–1–2.

Offenses try to exploit the defense by using set plays, patterns, or formations that attempt to mismatch or overload a given area of the court. The **passing game, high post/low post, shuffle offense,** and **single-post offense** are examples of offenses that work against man-to-man defenses. The use of **screens, give-and-go's,** and the **pick-and-roll** are maneuvers regularly found in man-to-man offenses.

Zone offenses attempt to use quick ball movement and mismatched positioning to gain position in the defense's protected areas. Mismatching means using offensive formations that overload a particular area against a zone defense or require the defense to decide how to defend one offensive player when two defensive players are available. An example of this is the use of a 1–3–1 offensive formation against a 2–1–2 defense.

PARTICIPANTS

zone defense *a defensive system in which each player is responsible for an assigned area of the court*

passing game *a type of offense in which players seem to move in a free-lance manner, but follow a set of rules*

high post *an offensive player who plays near the free throw line*

Basketball is a great game because it can easily be modified to account for any number of participants available at a given time. Official rules for basketball require five players per team on the court. Traditionally, these players have been known as **forward** (2), **guard** (2), and a **center.** In today's terminology, the players often are designated by name and a number system. The forwards are referred to as **small forward,** or #3 and **power forward,** or #4. A small forward (#3) usually is considered to be a good scorer (shooter), can potentially handle the ball from the perimeter, and usually faces the basket when making offensive moves with or without the ball. A power forward (#4), in contrast, is expected to be an aggressive rebounder on both offense and defense. This player's scoring opportunities usually are designed to come from offensive rebounds or from pick-and-roll plays with the #4 player generally setting the screens. Both #3 and #4 players are responsible for rebounding and filling a lane during a fast break.

The two guards are the #1, or **point guard,** and #2, or **shooting guard,** players. The point guard (#1) is charged with "running the offense." This means that this individual tends to be the best ball handler, has the ball in his/her possession a good deal of the time, and is responsible for getting the ball in the hands of the team's scorers at the appropriate time. The point guard (#1) usually leads the fast break and often is the first defender back in transition.

The shooting guard (#2) often is the best shooter from the perimeter of a team's offense. A good #2 player should be able to score consistently from the 18–22-feet range, fill a lane during the fast break, and get most of the long rebounds.

Finally, the center, or #5 player, is responsible primarily for inside scoring (around the basket), rebounding, and shot blocking. The center often begins offense play with his/her back to the basket, thus requiring the center to learn pivot player or big player skills and footwork. Generally, the center is the trailer during the fast break and protects the basket on defense.

In today's game, the size of the player doesn't always indicate the position that he/she will play. The power forwards (#4) and center (#5) most often are the taller, bigger players. Teams usually try to position players according to skills and physical talents rather than mere height.

A team is made up of eight to twelve players, although only five are on the court at one time. Most teams use seven to nine players regularly and develop a system of rotation when using substitutes. The sixth man, or first substitute, has become an important player in today's game and often logs more actual playing time than some starters.

Basketball can be played without following official rules for participants. Three-on-three basketball has become popular, and three-on-three tournaments are held regularly. There are age-group and skill-group divisions for both men and women. These games utilize only half a court (half-court games), and teams share a common basket. The rules also are modified for this variation of basketball.

Coaches often design drills and learning situations utilizing fewer than 10 players (5 per team). One-on-one games are common both in organized settings and on driveways throughout the United States. In fact, two-on-two, three-on-three, and four-on-four games probably are played more often than regulation five-on-five games. Finally, basketball skills can be developed alone. An individual can learn virtually every skill on his/her own if the situation requires this approach.

low post an offensive player who plays near the basket with his or her back to the basket

shuffle offense a continuity offense that requires each player to play all positions

single-post offense an offensive formation in which one player is stationed at either high or low post

screen a maneuver the offense uses in an effort to free a player for a shot at the basket; the screener stands in such a position that the opposing defensive player cannot get to the player who is in position to shoot

give-and-go passing the ball to a teammate and cutting hard to the basket for a return pass

pick and roll an offensive technique in which a player screens for a teammate who has the ball, and then rolls or moves to the basket for a pass

forward an offensive player who is stationed in the forecourt near the sideline toward the corner

guard an offensive position located away from the basket toward the center line

center a position usually played by the tallest player on the team, in charge of rebounding, shot blocking, and inside scoring

small forward an offensive player who usually is a good shooter and ball handler from the perimeter

power forward an offensive player who is an aggressive rebounder and usually scores from pick and rolls or offensive rebounds

point guard an offensive player who is the main ball handler and passes the ball to team scorers

shooting guard an offensive player who usually is the best shooter on the team

GAME ACTION

Basketball is started with a jump ball (discussed below) between any two of the opponents at center court. Upon gaining possession of the ball, each team strives to score or make baskets worth two or three points. At the same time, the opposing team is attempting to

turnover *loss of possession of the ball through error or a minor violation of the rules*

out of bounds *the area outside of the boundary lines*

foul *an infraction of the rules, usually because of contact between opposing players, for which one or more free throws are awarded or ball possession is lost*

gain possession of the ball by stealing it from the opponents, by way of a **turnover,** or from a defensive rebound or pressed shot from the opponents. The least acceptable method of gaining possession of the ball is when the opposing team successfully makes a shot or free throw. When this happens, the ball is put into play from behind the opponent's basket from the out-of-bounds area.

A player is **out-of-bounds** if he/she touches the floor on, or outside of, the boundary lines that surround the court. If the ball goes on or beyond the boundary lines as a result of a player's action, the opposing team puts the ball back into play from that point.

Basketball is fast-paced, with teams going from one end of the court to the other end with rapid transitions from offense to defense and vice versa. Action is slowed only when fouls or rule violations occur. Officials call a **foul** for any rule infraction that involves contact between opposing players. College men and women play two 20-minute halves with a 15-minute intermission. If the score is tied at the end of the 40 minutes, 5-minute periods are played until the tie is broken.

RULES

National Federation of State High Schools Association *governing organization that establishes rules for high school basketball play*

Federation Internationale de Basketball (FIBA) *organization that establishes international rules for basketball events such as the Olympics*

violation *an infringement of the rules in sports that is less serious than a foul and usually involves technicalities of play resulting in loss of possession of the ball*

The rules of basketball are determined by the organization or governing body for each level of play. High schools play by rules established by the **National Federation of State High Schools Association.** The National Collegiate Athletic Association (NCAA) establishes rules for college men and women. The National Basketball Association (NBA) governs professional players in the NBA. Finally, international rules for events such as the Olympics are established by the **Federation Internationale de Basketball (FIBA).** Although most rules at each of these levels are standardized, some differences in rules are designed to enhance the performance of play at that level.

For teaching and coaching purposes, rules can be modified for any level to help players learn skills, strategies, and concepts. Modifying equipment and rules for children is especially appropriate as they begin to learn the game of basketball.

The following major rules, fouls, and **violations** are for college men's and women's programs, with the differences pointed out and the most misunderstood rules examined.

MAJOR RULE VIOLATIONS FOR MEN'S AND WOMEN'S BASKETBALL

1. Stepping out-of-bounds with the ball or otherwise causing the ball to go out of bounds
2. Staying in one's own free throw lane for more than 3 seconds
3. Failure to inbound the ball within 5 seconds
4. Taking more than one step with the ball without passing, dribbling, or shooting
5. Double dribbling
6. Over-and-back-moving the ball into the back court once it has been advanced to the front court (men only)
7. Kicking the ball
8. Free throw lane violations such as stepping into the lane before the ball leaves the shooter's hand
9. Fouling the opponent

technical foul *a foul by either a player or a non-player that does not involve contact or that may involve unsportsmanlike acts with an opponent or official*

   a. **Technical fouls** can be assessed against court players, bench players, and coaches. Examples of technical fouls are unsportsmanlike conduct, taking more time-outs than are allotted, illegal touching of the rim or backboard, illegal substitution, and illegal uniforms. Technical fouls on court players result in one free throw and the opponent's possession of the ball. A technical foul on a coach or the bench results in two free throws and ball posses-sion for the opponents.

b. **Personal fouls** include holding, pushing, blocking, charging, hacking, or tripping an opponent. Any contact by a player that inhibits the freedom of movement of another player is a personal foul. Each player can continue to play with four or fewer personal fouls but must leave the game if he/she receives a fifth foul.

personal foul a foul caused by contact with an opponent while the ball is alive

Technical fouls count against players' personal foul total. When a foul is committed, the opponent may get to shoot free throws, take the ball out-of-bounds, or in the case of a technical foul, both. When a player is fouled in the act of shooting, he or she automatically gets two free throws. Otherwise, if the total team fouls are seven or fewer, the opponent takes the ball out of bounds. If the team total is seven to nine fouls, a player shoots one free throw and may shoot a second one if he/she makes the first one. If he/she misses the first free throw, the ball is in play for either team. If ten team fouls or more are assessed, the opponent receives two free throws.

If a violation is committed, the ball is given to the opponents out-of-bounds. When this happens, the violating team has committed a turnover.

MAJOR RULE DIFFERENCES BETWEEN COLLEGE MEN'S AND WOMEN'S BASKETBALL

1. Women use a 30-second shot clock. This clock requires the offensive team to attempt a shot and make contact with the rim within this timeframe. If a shot is not taken or the ball has not touched the rim within 30 seconds of posses-sion, an alarm sounds and the offensive team must give up possession of the ball. College men use a 35-second shot clock. The same rules apply, but the time is different.

2. A men's offensive team must advance the ball from its back court to its front court within 10 seconds after gaining possession of the ball inbound. Once front court is established, the offense cannot return to its back court unless the defensive team causes the ball to go there.

RULE VIOLATIONS THAT COLLEGE FANS OFTEN MISUNDERSTAND

1. *Over-and-back.* An offensive player is not considered to have entered the front court until both the entire body and the ball have touched the front court. It is possible for the ball to remain in the back court after the body has crossed the mid-court line, or vice versa. A player also may step over the mid-court line with one foot and then return that same foot to the back court without violation.

2. *Charging.* In **charging,** the player that is charged into must first establish court position before the opponent. This does not always mean that the player has to be completely stationary, though. The official must decide which player has established position on the court first. As an example, a defender is backpedaling and an offensive player runs over him. The defender was moving but clearly had gained that court position first; therefore, a charge is called on the offensive player.

charging running into a player who is stationary or has an established position

3. *Blocking.* A defender may not make contact with an airborne offensive player or move into this offensive player's path and become stationary if the offensive player has already left the floor. The defense must allow the offense to "come down." Many fans see a stationary defender hit by an airborne offender and assume that a charge will be called, but an official will call a block if the defender moved to this position after the offensive player had taken flight.

blocking positioning of a defensive player in a manner so as to prevent an offensive player from establishing court position

4. *Kicked ball.* Kicking the ball with the foot or lower leg is illegal. The act of kicking, however, must be considered intentional by the official before a kick is called. An example of a non-kick or no-call is the case where the ball deflects off a dribbler's leg. This is not an intentional kick, so no call is made. Also, a defender might come into contact with a loose ball that inadvertently touches his/her foot or leg. This is not a kicked ball if the official believes the defender had no intention to stop or deflect the ball.

THE COURT, BACKBOARD, AND BASKETS

The playing court in college men's and women's basketball is 94 feet by 50 feet. Figure 2.1 shows dimensions and markings for the rectangular playing surface.

The court is divided into symmetrical halves by the mid-court line. Each half court has a rectangular backboard measuring 6 feet (1.83m) wide and 4 feet (1.23m) high, located at the center of each end of the court 4 feet (1.23m) in from the baseline and 9 feet (2.74m) above the floor. A rectangular box is centered on the backboard. This box is 18 inches vertically and 24 inches horizontally behind the metal ring suspended from the backboard.

Figure 2.1

Dimensions and markings of a basketball court.

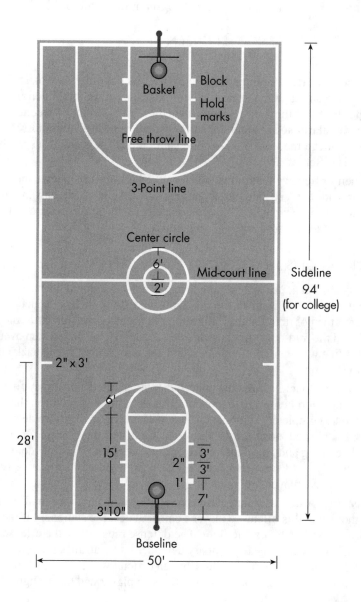

The basket is an open hammock net on an 18-inch-diameter metal ring, which must be 6 inches from the rigid surface to which it is fastened and 10 feet (3.05m) above the floor. Each basket area contains the free throw lane area or *key.* The lane is bordered by the baseline at the end of the court and the free throw line at the top of the key. The lane lines are 12 feet (3.66m) apart and contain the block and hash marks that represent player areas for free throw attempts. During a free throw, players from the defensive team must occupy both lane spaces adjacent to the baseline.

The free throw line is 15 feet (4.57m) from the basket and 18 feet 10 inches (5.74m) from the baseline. A circle with a 6-foot (1.83m) radius goes around the free throw line. This free throw circle is marked with a broken line in the lane semicircle and a solid line forms the semicircle above the free throw line. A 3-point line is 19 feet 9 inches (6m) from the basket. This line touches the top of the free throw circle and arcs toward the sideline and eventually touches the baseline.

The mid-court line dissects the center circle. This circle is the area where the start of a game or the start of an overtime period commences. Here, two players execute a **jump ball** or try to tap the ball to one of their teammates.

jump ball the situation resolving joint possession, in which the official tosses the ball into the air and two opposing players jump in an effort to tap the ball toward a teammate

SCORING

A **field goal** is scored when a shot enters the basket from above and passes down through it. A field goal from behind the 3-point line counts 3 points. Any field goal from the 3-point line itself to all others from closer range counts 2 points. If a player makes a field goal in the opponent's basket, the points are awarded to the opponent.

Scoring can also occur by way of a free throw shot (discussed later). One point is awarded for each successful free throw shot.

ETIQUETTE

1. *Formal etiquette.* A summary of the prominent items includes the following:
   a. There is to be no talking or waving of body parts during the execution of a free throw.
   b. Players are expected to respect officials and show courtesy to opponents at all times.
   c. Visible displays of anger or inappropriate language toward officials is considered detrimental to the game, and a technical foul will be assessed.
   d. Fouls that are considered **flagrant,** unnecessarily rough, or perceived to intentionally put the opponent in danger of physical harm are treated as dirty play. The offending player will be assessed appropriate fouls (technical or personal) and may be subject to ejection from the game.
2. *Informal etiquette.* All players should display sportsmanlike behavior and etiquette to ensure the safety and enjoyment of all involved.
   a. Many basketball games are played without officials. In these instances, the players must police themselves. Any player can call a foul, but those who foul should call the foul on themselves. This will help keep the game honest and free of controversy.
   b. Basketball is a team game, so the interests of teammates should be a focal part of the game. Teammates' accomplishments should be recognized, and blaming teammates for failures is to be avoided.
   c. A humble player is gracious in both defeat and victory and avoids calling attention to himself/herself in ways other than quality play.

field goal a score that is valued at 2 or 3 points, depending on the distance from where the ball is launched, and is awarded to a player who shoots the ball over the rim and through the net

flagrant foul a foul intended to harm the opponent

Skills and Drills

Sound fundamentals are necessary in the making of good basketball players. Through the years, basketball coaching legends such as Bee, Rupp, Auerbach, Wooden, Winters, Smith, Knight, and Krzyzewski have continuously stressed and taught the fundamental skills of basketball. Section 3 covers skills that are considered essential in providing a basic framework for the development of fundamentally sound basketball players.

Fundamental skills are divided into three areas: *individual offensive skills, transition skills,* and *individual defensive skills.*

FUNDAMENTAL BASKETBALL SKILLS

Individual Offense Skills

To play offense, a basketball player must be able to handle the ball in a variety of ways, as well as learn to move the body quickly and purposefully to help his/her team score points. First and foremost, *ball-handling skills* are essential to efficient execution of all facets of offensive play in the game of basketball. *Passing, receiving,* and *dribbling* skills are the primary ball-handling skills. These skills allow for successful movement of the ball from one end of the court to the other and for execution of set offensive plays.

Individual offensive skills also encompass body-control fundamentals. *Pivoting, faking,* and *cutting* are required of all players for the execution of ball-handling skills, shooting skills, and set offensive play.

The successful completion of offense is defined by the awarding of 1, 2, or 3 points upon making a basket. Therefore, *shooting* skills are necessary for a "happy ending" to offensive play.

Transition Skills

In many ways, the essence of basketball is the ability of one team to take advantage of the other team. In today's game many advantages can be gained using fundamental transition skills. The player must learn to *rebound* missed shot from both an *offensive* and a *defensive* perspective. Offensive rebounds allow a team a second chance to score immediately or to set up the offense to execute successful plays. Defensive rebounds can lead to fast-break opportunities. *Fast breaks* are often the result of defensive rebounds and the beginning of offensive play. Transition skills from defense to offense or from offense back to defense enable players to quickly adapt to today's fast paced game.

In addition, properly controlling loose or free balls can lead to an easy basket or can save a possession. Therefore, gaining possession of any ball that either team is not controlling is important in allowing transitional play to be an advantage in the game of basketball.

Individual Defense Skills

The most fundamental and important skills to master are those of *individual defense.* Team defense is only as good as the defense of each team member. Therefore, to play good defense, all players must develop footwork, positioning, and mental skills.

This section is concerned primarily with fundamental individual skills for all aspects of team basketball. Team offensive and defensive strategies are covered in Section 4.

INDIVIDUAL OFFENSE SKILLS
Ball-Handling Skills

The individual offensive skills included in this section are ball-handling skills:

- Passing
- Receiving
- Dribbling

Passing is the most important offensive fundamental skill in basketball. Passing moves the ball from player to player, from one end of the court to the other, and from one spot on the court to another. All plays are grounded in efficient movement of the ball, and passing is the quickest, most efficient way to move the ball in basketball. Passes included in this section are: chest, bounce, two-handed overhead, baseball, flip, and one-handed push pass.

Receiving or catching the ball requires good hands, anticipation, and concentration. The player without the ball is always a potential receiver; therefore, he/she always must maintain eye contact with the ball. A player must catch the ball before it can be passed or shot again.

Dribbling tends to be the most overused and improperly used skill in basketball. Still, dribbling is an important part of ball handling. The dribble can be used to position the ball on the court, to escape trouble, and to advance the ball when a pass is not possible. The controlled dribble, speed dribble, cross-over dribble, and behind-the-back dribble are discussed in this section. Table 3.1 provides a summary of the ball-handling skills.

TABLE 3.1	Ball-handling skills: Summary table.	
SKILL	**TYPES**	**USES**
PASSING	Chest	1. For distances up to 20 feet
		2. Best used when defensive pressure is light
	One-handed Push Pass	1. To advance the ball down the court
		2. To initiate offense
		3. To hit cutters
	Bounce	1. To pass under or around defensive man
		2. To pass to pivot players or cutters
	Two-handed Overhead	1. Used as a skip pass
		2. Used after defensive rebounds
		3. To initiate set offense
		4. To hit cutters
		5. Used by players who have just received a high pass and want to make a quick return pass
	Flip (Hand-off)	1. Used in close quarters
		2. Used by post players passing to cutters
	Baseball	1. Long, lead pass—half court to full court in length
		2. Used after defensive rebounds
		3. Used for inbound plays from back court
DRIBBLING	Controlled Dribble	1. To advance the ball when time is not a factor
		2. To get out of trouble when passing is not possible
		3. To drive by a defensive player on a move to the basket
	Speed Dribble	1. To advance the ball quickly up court on a break or steal
		2. Best used when the distance between the ball handler and the defense is the same
	Cross-over Dribble	1. To switch the ball to the other hand
		2. To change directions quickly
		3. To elude a defender
		4. To protect the ball
	Behind-the-back Dribble	1. To switch the ball to the other hand
		2. To elude a defender
		3. To protect the ball
		4. To change directions quickly

SKILL 1 Passing

Passing fundamentals often are considered the most important skills to learn in team-oriented offensive basketball. Many different types of passes have been taught and utilized through the years.

All passes require adept handling of the ball. Some essentials are as follows.

1. The ball should be controlled by the fingertips and, though some contact is inevitable, the ball should not be resting in the palms or heels of the hands.
2. The fingers should be spread and a wrist snap should be stressed.
3. All passes require follow-through.
4. Passes should be on the side away from the defensive player.
5. Timing and accuracy are crucial.
6. Passes should be fast and crisp.
7. The speed of the pass depends upon the distance and speed of the receivers.
8. The player should not **telegraph** and, instead, should use **split vision.**
9. The simplest pass possible should be used to complete the play.
10. Passing is the fastest method of advancing the ball.

telegraph to let others know your intentions

split vision look one way, pass the other way

Passes discussed in this section are grouped according to type and use of each pass. The *chest pass,* the *one-handed push pass,* and the *bounce pass* are discussed together because of their similar characteristics with respect to execution. The *two-handed overhead pass* and the *flip pass* are discussed together because both usually are used during set offensive play. The final pass discussed is the *baseball pass,* which is used to advance the ball over longer distances, quickly.

Figure 3.1
Two-handed chest pass.

In two-handed chest pass:

- put backspin on ball
- extend elbows
- turn thumbs down
- release ball from fingertips
- move toward the receiver

Chest Pass

The chest pass is the pass to use whenever possible, as it is the quickest to advance the ball safely. It is best used for short distances of not more than 15 to 20 feet.

The ball should be held toward the rear of the ball with the fingers of both hands spread and the thumbs pointing inward. The ball is held chest high with the elbows close to the body. The ball is released with a wrist and finger snap with hands facing the floor. The follow-through involves both hands and one foot reaching toward the intended target. The decision of which foot to step forward should be based on situational factors and comfort for the passer. The ball should reach the receiver between the waist and the shoulders.

Unsuccessful chest passes usually produce turnovers and often result from poor judgment as to proper speed of the pass or of the receiver. Passes that are either below the waist or above the receiver's head are other common errors. Figure 3.1 illustrates the chest pass.

One-handed Push Pass

The one-handed push pass is much like the chest pass and embraces the same principles. The ball is held the same, but the ball is "pushed" from the dominant hand with the forearm, wrist, finger, and thumb snap. The other hand is used to hold and protect the ball much like the shooting motion.

Possible errors include a trajectory that is too high or too low or is difficult to receive. When executed properly, the one-handed push pass is the fastest in basketball.

Bounce Pass

The bounce pass may be executed like the two-handed chest pass. The hand positioning (fingers spread, thumbs inward), elbows close to the body, and follow-through are the same as the chest pass and the push pass. The wrist and finger snap, however, may require more force, and more body lean may be necessary to complete this type of pass successfully. The ball should strike the floor approximately two-thirds of the distance to the receiver and bounce so it is caught near the receiver's hip away from a defender. If the pass bounces too close to the receiver's feet, it will be difficult to catch. If it bounces too far from the receiver, it will arrive slowly and can be easily intercepted by the defense.

This pass is used for short distances to go under the defenders or into the **pivot** players. Because this pass tends to be slower than other types of passes, it should be used near the basket or when the receiver is going to dribble or throw a flip pass to a **cutter.** The bounce pass is illustrated in Figure 3.2.

Table 3.2 is a guide summarizing the chest, one-handed push, and bounce pass cues and errors.

Figure 3.2
Bounce pass.

pivot an offensive player position sometimes referred to as a post; usually, tall, strong rebounders who can pass and set screens play this position

cutter an offensive player who uses a quick movement to elude an opponent so he/she can receive a pass from a teammate while going to an open area on the court or when going toward the basket

TABLE 3.2   Chest, one-handed push, and bounce passes: Action, cues and troubleshooting.

*TYPE OF PASS	BIOMECHANICAL ACTIONS	VERBAL CUES	ERRORS	CAUSES OF ERRORS

*Chest Pass
 	
*One-Handed Push Pass
 	
*Bounce Pass
	■ Fingers spread
	■ Thumbs on ball pointing inward
	■ Ball held chest high
	■ Wrist and finger snap
	■ Follow-through
	  a. one- or two-handed
	  b. one foot
		■ Spread fingers
		■ Thumbs down
		■ Snap wrist
		■ Reach with arms
		■ Step
		■ Target: chest (bounce-hip)
			1. Pass too high or too low to catch
			
			2. Pass too slow or too fast to catch
			
			3. Pass on defender's side
				1. Bounced too close to receiver
				
				2. No wrist snap No follow-through
				
				3. Misjudged speed of receiver

*Biomechanical Actions, Verbal Cues, Errors, and Causes of Errors apply to each type of pass.

Passing Drills

The following drills are intended to be *sequential* for learning the *chest, one-handed push,* and *bounce* passes. Drill #1 is a partner drill with a stationary target. Drill #2 continues with a stationary target but adds players to the drill to move from partner to small group or team practice. The third and fourth drills continue group practice, but a moving target is added in the sequence. Therefore, these four drills move the practice of each pass from simple form and accuracy into team and gamelike situations.

Drill #1: Partner Pass Drill

The Partner Pass Drill (Figure 3.3) consists of two players (partners) simply passing back and forth, working together on execution, form, and accuracy of each pass. If a partner is not available, an individual player can practice these passes with the use of a throw-back device or against a wall.

CUES: 1. Spread fingers
2. Snap wrist
3. Reach with arms and one foot to target

Drill #2: Diamond Passing Drill

CUES: 1. Spread fingers
2. Snap wrist
3. Reach with arms and one foot to target

In the Diamond Passing Drill (Figure 3.4), X_1 passes to X_2 and breaks fast to the right and to the rear of the line headed by X_2. X_2 passes to X_3 and breaks fast to the

Figure 3.3 (on left)
Partner pass drill.

Figure 3.4 (on right)
Diamond passing drill.

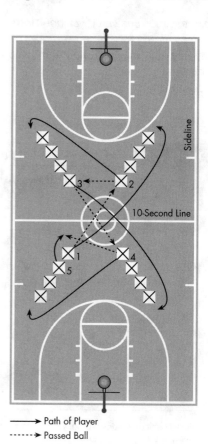

rear of that line. X₃ passes to X₄ and breaks fast to the left and to the rear of that line. X₄ passes to X₅ and breaks left to the rear of that line. The drill continues in this fashion as long as desired. *Note:* The corners can be backed up to teach longer passes.

Drill #3: Four-Corner Passing Drill

Once the technique and execution of each pass is understood, the passes in most passing drills should be made from moving players or after coming to a quick stop to moving receivers or to receivers in their normal offensive positions. Passing should be learned in the context of gamelike play and practice. Figure 3.5 illustrates the four-corner passing drill.

CUES: 1. Lead the receiver
2. Target is chest (hip for bounce pass)
3. Follow through

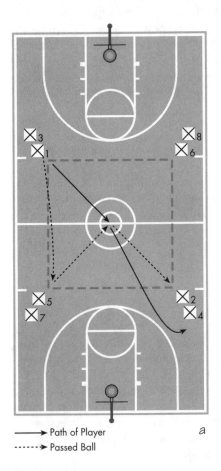

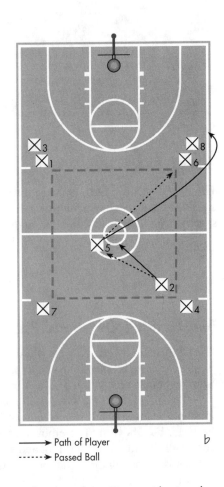

Figure 3.5

Four-corner passing drill.

X₁ passes to X₅, cuts on a diagonal, receiving the pass from X₅ at midpoint, then passes to X₂ and goes to the end of that line.

X₅, after passing to X₁, cuts on a diagonal, receives a pass from X₂, then passes to X₆ and goes to the end of that line. The player passes, receives the pass, makes a pass and then goes to the end of the line where he/she last passed.

X₅, X₆, X₇, and X₈ always stay in the same line as do X₁, X₂, X₃, and X₄. The player runs across in a straight line. He/she should wait for the ball in his/her corner to come to him/her. At first, one ball is used in this drill. However, a second and third ball can be added to increase the complexity of the drill.

Figure 3.6

Pass and move drill.

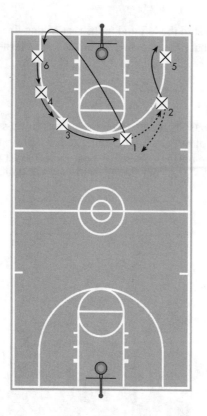

→ Path of Player

- - -> Path of Ball

X1 passes to X2, and moves to position X6 originally occupied, X3 fills in X1's original position; as he/she does so, X4 fills in original position of X3. X2 passes to X3 as he/she comes to the position originally occupied by X1. X2 then moves to position X5 originally occupied. At the same time, X3 passes to X4 as he/she moves up to fill the X3 spot. This passing and filling spots continues throughout the drill. *Note:* The passer can go to any of the other positions he/she desires, and when he/she vacates the position he/she is in, the nearest player without the ball must fill in quickly.

Drill #4: Pass and Move Drill

The Pass and Move Drill (see Figure 3.6) emphasizes the importance of maintaining floor balance when a player passes and moves to another position. Fifteen-foot spacing should be maintained throughout the drill.

CUES: 1. Maintain 15-foot spacing
2. Target chest or hip
3. Follow through

Two-Handed Overhead Pass

The two-handed overhead pass (Figure 3.7) is excellent in initiating a set offense. It can be used to hit pivot players, to pass to cutters, or to quickly return a high pass just caught by a receiver. It also can be used to begin the fast break.

The hands are on the sides of the ball with the fingers pointed upward and the thumbs pointing inward toward each other. The ball should be slightly in front of the head, but above it. The elbows are slightly bent, and the pass is executed by stepping forward with either foot and snapping the wrist and fingers, with the palm and hands following through in a downward position.

An effective two-handed overhead pass will follow a quick path on a high plane for a distance of 15 to 20 feet. If the distance is too long or a quick, firm wrist and finger snap is not executed, the ball will result in an arched or lobbed pass that can be easily intercepted.

CUES: 1. Hands on side of ball
2. Ball slightly in front but above head
3. Elbows slightly bent
4. Step forward (either foot)
5. Snap wrist and fingers downward

Flip Pass

The flip pass is a short, quick pass used primarily in give-and-go tactics. It is often used by pivot players hitting cutters in close quarters.

Using both hands, the pass is "flipped" by the wrists with the fingers and hands (not arms) extended on the follow-through. It should not be thrown toward a receiver or merely dropped. It should be received at waist level, however, and basically remain on the same plane from which it was passed for a distance of two or three feet. The ball should be protected by having the elbows out and the body in a crouched position.

The ball is not thrown or handed to the receiver. Errors result when the ball is not flipped by the wrists and fingers of both hands along the same path as the receiver's waist level. Also, errors or fumbles can occur when the passer does not protect the ball with his/her body and elbows.

Table 3.3 summarizes the cues and errors of the two-handed overhead pass and the flip pass.

Passing Drills, *continued*

The following drills can be used to practice the two-handed overhead pass. The drills are sequential and progress from a partner, emphasizing form and accuracy, to more complex, gamelike situations. This progression generally introduces more passers or a defensive player(s).

Drill #5: Partner Pass Drill (see Drill #1)

The Partner Pass Drill can be utilized to practice most types of passes.

Drill #6: Triangle Pass Drill

In the Triangle Pass, the players divide into groups of three; each group forms a triangle with the players about 15 feet apart (Figure 3.8). The ball is moved quickly between players and the direction is changed frequently.

CUES: 1. Quick, firm wrist and finger snap
2. Hold ball above head with elbows slightly bent
3. Follow through extending hands and arms in high plane along path of the ball

Note: The chest, one-handed push, and bounce passes can also be practiced using this drill.

Drill #7: Pass to Post Drill

The Pass to Post Drill (Figure 3.9) allows for practice of passes into the post, which is the primary use of the two-handed overhead pass. X_1 passes to X_2 by going over O_1. The defensive player may not be used initially but should be added to make this practice more gamelike.

Figure 3.7
Two-handed overhead pass.

Ball high above head, released with a flick of the wrists

Figure 3.8
Triangle pass drill.

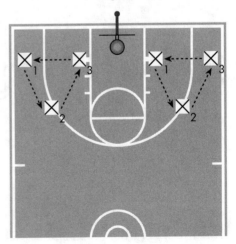

------► Passed Ball

TABLE 3.3 Two-handed overhead and flip passes: Action, cues, and troubleshooting.

TYPE OF PASS	BIOMECHANICAL ACTIONS	VERBAL CUES	ERRORS	CAUSES OF ERRORS
Two-Handed Overhead	■ Hands on side of ball; fingers upward; thumbs inward toward each other ■ Elbows slightly bent; ball held in front but above head ■ Forward step (either foot) ■ Wrist and fingers snapped; follow through with palms and hands in downward position	■ Hands at sides ■ Hold above head with elbows slightly bent ■ Snap wrist and fingers ■ Follow through with hands and arms extended in high plane or path of ball	1. Ball is lobbed 2. Ball is passed too low	1. Ball should remain on a fairly high plane; if wrist and finger snap are not firm and quick or if distance of pass is too long, a lob pass is likely to occur 2. Plane or path of ball is abruptly changed by an exaggerated (downward) follow-through
Flip	■ With both hands on ball, flip wrists ■ Fingers and hands (not arms) extended ■ Ball protected with elbows out, body crouched	■ Flip wrists ■ Follow through with hands	1. Slow pass 2. Dropped too high or too low to catch 3. Pass deflected	1. Not flipped directly to receiver's hands 2. Ball didn't remain in same plane as it started (wrist level) 3. Ball not protected by elbows and body

Figure 3.9
Pass to post drill.

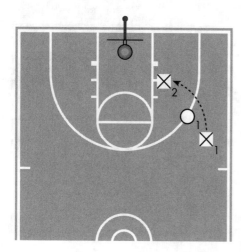

------▶ Passed Ball

Practicing the flip pass follows a sequence similar to the two-handed overhead pass drill. This pass is used in the pivot offense in feeding cutters off the post. Therefore, this pass naturally follows the two-handed overhead pass in the post as a sequential progression for offensive play.

CUES: 1. Hold ball high
2. Snap wrists and fingers
3. Utilize two-handed overhead fake

Drill #8: Short Exchange Drill

In the Short Exchange Drill (Figure 3.10), X₁ makes a flip pass to X₂ who is cutting in front of X₁. X₁ then goes to the end of line B and X₂ flip passes to X₃ cutting in front and goes to the end of line A. The drill then continues in this manner.

CUES: 1. Flip wrists

2. Ball should travel directly to receiver's hands (waist level)

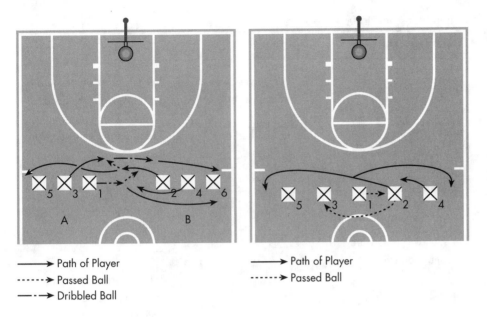

→ Path of Player
--→ Passed Ball
—·→ Dribbled Ball

→ Path of Player
--→ Passed Ball

Figure 3.10 (on left)
Short exchange drill.

Figure 3.11 (on right)
Five-player weave half court drill.

X₁ flip passes to X₂ and goes in front of X₂ as X₂ is moving toward X₁. X₁ then runs to the sideline and returns. X₂ passes to X₃ and goes in front of X₃ on the way to the sideline and returns. X₃ passes, goes in front of X₄, continues to the sideline, and so on. This process continues until the coach/teacher indicates a change.

Drill #9: Five-Player Weave Half Court Drill

The Five-Player Weave Half Court Drill (Figure 3.11) utilizes the same concepts as the Short Exchange (Drill 8) but involves only five players and is continuous.

CUES: 1. Flip wrists
2. Meet the ball
3. Go in front of receiver

Baseball Pass

Baseball passes (see Figure 3.12) are useful for long lead passes and for getting the ball away from the defensive boards quickly. They are often used in fast break situations and against pressing tactics, when distance and speed are especially important.

The passer holds the ball high above the side of the head with the passing hand behind the ball and fingers spread comfortably. The non-throwing hand should be in front of the ball to help control and balance it.

This pass resembles the type of throw that a baseball catcher uses to throw to second base. The ball is thrown with the passing hand only. The passing arm is bent at the elbow and pulled back. The weight of the body shifts to the passing side, and the free arm is extended forward for balance.

When the ball is thrown, the fingers and hand should face inward on the follow-through. The wrist must snap straight so the ball has a true reverse spin. The ball should be released on a high plane. As the throwing arm is brought forward, the opposite foot steps forward and the weight is shifted to it as the foot lands. As the ball is released, the foot on the passing hand side swings into position even with the front foot. The head should be up before releasing the ball.

Throwing errors occur if the passer begins to run before completely releasing the ball or applies side spin to the ball by twisting the hand as it releases the ball. Side spin is undesirable because the

Figure 3.12
Baseball pass.

With the baseball pass:

- Shift weight to the front foot as you step toward receiver
- Snap your wrist—the ball is released off of fingertips

TABLE 3.4 Baseball pass: Action, cues and troubleshooting.

BIOMECHANICAL ACTION	VERBAL CUES	ERRORS	CAUSE OF ERRORS
■ Ball is held high above side of head with fingers of passing hand spread	■ Hold ball high with both hands	1. Ball curves away from receiver	1. Ball gets side spin because of much twisting of the hand
■ Non-throwing hand is placed in front of ball	■ Step forward on foot opposite throwing hand	2. Ball is short of receiver	2. Passer doesn't shift weight to front foot
■ Passing arm is bent at elbow and pulled back	■ Lead with non-throwing hand		*or*
■ As throwing arm moves forward, non-throwing hand is extended forward for balance	■ Shift weight forward and snap wrist		Passer begins to run before releasing ball
	■ Follow through		*or*
■ Weight of body is on passing side; opposite foot steps forward and weight shifts to it as the foot lands			Passer doesn't follow through or doesn't release ball on a high plane
■ Wrist snaps straight as fingers and hands face inward on follow-through			
■ Ball is released on high plane			

ball tends to curve and may jeopardize the accuracy of the pass. A spinning ball also is more difficult to catch.

Hint: To avoid a curve ball, follow through with the throwing hand's *palm facing out.*

Table 3.4 provides a guide for form, cues, and troubleshooting for the base-ball pass.

Passing Drills, *continued*

Drill #10: Baseball Pass Drill

In the Baseball Pass Drill (Figure 3.13), two players start 20 feet apart. The players play catch, throwing back and forth easily. The distance and speed are increased as the players become comfortable and accurate with this pass. A distance of the length of the full court could be practiced if desired.

CUES: 1. Hold ball high with both hands
2. Step forward on foot opposite throwing hand
3. Shift weight forward and snap wrist

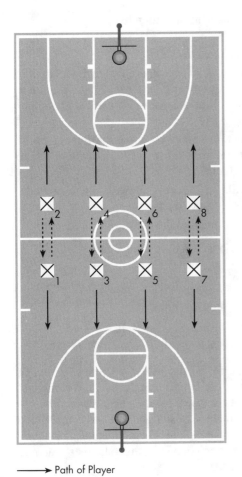

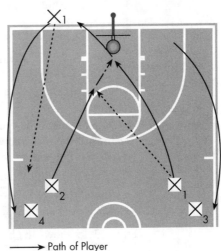

→ Path of Player
- - -→ Passed Ball
— · -→ Dribbled Ball

→ Path of Player
- - -→ Passed Ball

Drill #11: Break-away Drill

Figure 3.14 illustrates the Break-away Drill as follows:

X_1 passes to X_2 as he/she makes a cut to the basket. X_2 catches the pass and shoots a lay-up shot. X_1 follows the shot, steps out of bounds, and passes to X_4 at half court, and follows the pass to the end of this line. X_2 passes to X_3, and the drill continues. The distance can be increased or decreased as appropriate.

CUES: 1. Hold ball high
2. Step forward on foot opposite throwing arm
3. Snap wrist and shift weight forward

SKILL 2 Receiving the Ball

Receiving or catching the ball is just as important as learning different types of passes. Indeed, many so-called passing errors or mistakes are the result of the receiving player's making an error rather than the passer's making a bad pass. All players are potential receivers and should know where the ball is at all times. Receiving the ball requires the player to:

1. Keep hands above the waist with fingers spread and relaxed while giving the passer a wide palm target on the side away from the defense.
2. Hold hands in a funnel-shaped position reaching toward an incoming pass.

Figure 3.15

Receiving the pass.

When receiving a pass:

- Follow the ball with your eyes
- Block with right hand and tuck left hand
- Relax and spread fingers

3. Catch the ball by the fingertips and thumbs.

4. Recoil the wrists and elbows upon impact to absorb the force of the ball or "catch using soft-hands."

5. For a pass that is waist-high or above, point the fingers up, the palms forward, and the thumbs in. For a pass below the waist, point the fingers down with the palms forward and thumbs out.

6. Move toward the ball when receiving a pass. Often, stepping toward the ball allows the receiver to use the body and feet to protect the path of the ball.

7. Upon receiving the ball, use the arms immediately to carry the ball into a position for a shot or a pass.

8. Keep eyes on the ball throughout the catch.

Figure 3.15 shows the body position to receive a pass.

CUES:
1. Provide a target
2. Reach and step toward incoming pass
3. Catch with fingers and thumb
4. Use "soft-hands" to absorb impact
5. Keep eyes on the ball

All potential receivers should be anticipating the ball at all times. Errors or fumbles occur from receivers' not being alert and expecting the ball and receivers' taking their eyes off the ball in an attempt to shoot, pass, dribble, or turn before gaining possession. Other receiving errors include misjudging the pass, not having the hands up and ready, running away from the ball, and being mentally or physically tired. Table 3.5 summarizes the pass-receiving fundamentals, lists teaching cues, and gives possible errors and their causes.

The following passing and receiving drills are included to further develop fundamental passing and receiving skills. Any pass may be used.

Passing and Receiving Drills

Drill #12: Split-vision Drill

In the Split-vision Drill (Figure 3.16), one player with a ball stands in front of a group stationed in a row in such a way that each may receive a pass. A second ball is located at the end of the group line. The two balls are passed back and forth, up and down in the line. Players rotate so each stands in front of the group.

CUES:
1. Give a target
2. Reach for pass
3. Catch with fingers

Drill #13: Three-Player Full Court Passing Drill

The sequence described in Figure 3.17 is used in the Three-Player Full Court Passing Drill.

CUES:
1. Give target
2. Lead the receiver
3. Use soft hands

Figure 3.16

Split-vision drill.

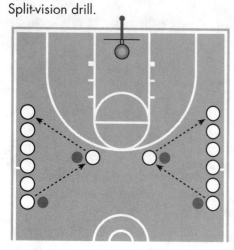

------▶ Passed Ball

TABLE 3.5	Receiving a pass: Action, cues, and troubleshooting.		
BIOMECHANICAL ACTION	**VERBAL CUES**	**ERRORS**	**CAUSES OF ERRORS**
■ Hands are held above the waist with fingers spread while giving a target	■ Provide a target	■ Fumbles	■ Not being alert and expecting the ball
■ Hands reach toward ball in a funnel-shaped position	■ Reach and step toward pass		■ Taking eyes off ball to make next move before gaining possession
■ Fingertips and thumbs meet the ball	■ Catch with fingers and thumbs		■ Misjudging the pass (spin, speed, etc.)
■ Wrists and elbows recoil to absorb impact	■ Use soft hands		
■ Player steps toward ball	■ Keep eyes on the ball		■ Running away from the ball
■ Hands adjust to height of pass; fingers and thumbs are up if ball is waist high or higher, down if below waist			■ Being mentally or physically tired

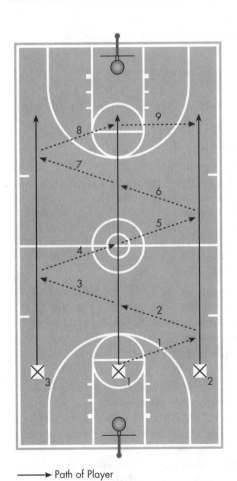

1. Set up three lines on the **baseline** with the ball in the middle.
2. X_1 passes to X_2 who passes back to X_1 who pivots and passes to the opposite lane, X_3.
3. Continue this movement going to the other end of the court and back.

baseline the end line running under the basket from sideline to sideline

Figure 3.17
Three-player full court passing drill.

→ Path of Player

----→ Passed Ball

SKILL 3 Dribbling

Dribbling is not just bouncing the ball. It is a part of ball handling. It is a highly skilled fundamental that requires players not only to control the ball well but also be totally aware of the positioning of teammates and defensive players. A good dribbler (ball handler) is an alert passer whose head is always up, who has wide vision to see the whole floor, and who doesn't look at the ball. Dribbling is a vital part of the game and an effective way to advance the ball. The dribble, however, should be used only when the player has a definite purpose.

The dribble has many uses, listed in the guidelines below.

1. Do not dribble when you can pass to a teammate.
2. Dribble when open for a short drive to the basket.
3. Dribble as a planned maneuver in a set offensive play, such as a screen or a player cutting behind the dribbler.
4. Dribble when advancing the ball to the front court in the fast break when there is no open player ahead or for a slow advance.
5. Dribble for a quick getaway with an intercepted pass.
6. Dribble to get away from the man-to-man pressing defense.
7. Dribble to get away from a pressing opponent under the defensive board and out of congested areas.
8. Dribble when teammates are covered; dribble to get in better position to pass.
9. Dribble with a specific purpose, not just bouncing the ball.
10. Keep the head up at all times and the ball close and under control.
11. Keep away from sidelines and corners.
12. When picking up the ball from the dribble, immediately pass or shoot, not just hold the ball and look.
13. Learn to control the ball with either hand, using the dominant hand when possible.

All players should learn the following types of dribbles: *controlled dribble, speed dribble,* and *cross-over dribble.* Players who will be primary ball handlers also may want to master the *behind-the-back dribble.* Finally, a good dribbler (ball handler) should be able not only to utilize these specific skills but also be able to change from one to another quickly and efficiently.

Controlled Dribble

The **controlled dribble** (Figure 3.18) is also known as a *low dribble.* The fingers are spread and the ball is pushed to the floor with the fingertip and a flip of the wrist. Slapping the ball or using the palms of the hands is inefficient and awkward. The hands are slightly cupped and the elbow is kept close to the body.

The ball should be to the side and slightly in front of the body. The knees should be bent with the back straight so the body is in a crouched position. The body is used to protect the ball by keeping it between the defender and the ball.

Because this is a low, controlled dribble, the ball should not come up higher than the knee. The closer the defense, the lower the dribble to make it difficult for the defender to flick away the ball. Finally, good dribblers keep their head up to see the positioning of their teammates and how the defense is set up.

Dribbling too high when being guarded closely, not putting the body between the ball and the defender, or not keeping the elbow in may result in having the ball stolen from the dribbler.

Figure 3.18 (on left)
Controlled dribble.

Figure 3.19 (on right)
Speed dribble.

When dribbling:
- Keep head up and knees flexed
- Use fingertip control
- Dribble low

With speed dribble:
- Keep head up
- Push ball with fingertips
- Body is erect with elbow out in front

Speed Dribble

The **speed dribble** (Figure 3.19) is used on a fast break or when a player is out in front of the defense. It also can be utilized when driving to the basket when in the open.

The ball is still pushed with the fingertips and with a flip of the wrist. The hands are still cupped, and the head is always up. But this dribble has important differences in execution, compared to the controlled dribble. First, the body is not as crouched. The ball is pushed out even more in front of the ball handler. The elbow, therefore, will be more out in front so the ball is pushed away from the dribbler. This allows for more speed, and the dribbler must run to meet the ball. Finally, the ball will rebound higher. Waist-high dribbles are appropriate, and dribbles that rebound too high should be given careful attention.

If the ball is dribbled too high or too low, the ball handler may have to slow down to gain control. Also, high dribbles are easier to flick away. Therefore, the advantage gained using the speed dribble may be lost by allowing the defense to catch up to the dribbler.

Cross-over Dribble

The **cross-over dribble** (Figure 3.20) usually is associated with a change of pace or direction and is used with either the controlled or the speed dribble previously discussed. The cross-over dribble means that the ball is switched quickly from one hand to the other as the ball passes in front of the body.

This quick switch is accomplished by flicking the ball on the outside so it bounces across in front of the body to the opposite hand. The ball should be close to the body as the weight shifts from one foot to the other. Because the ball passes between the defender and the dribbler, a quick, low dribble usually is required. The flicking hand and foot on the same side as the flicking hand also must cross over for protection.

speed dribble a dribble in which the body is upright and the ball is pushed out in front to advance the ball quickly downcourt

Figure 3.20
Cross-over dribble.

With cross-over dribble:
- Switch ball quickly from one hand to the other
- Ball is close to body as weight is shifted from one foot to the other

cross-over dribble *a dribble in which the ball is quickly switched from one hand to the other as the ball passes in front of the body*

The defense can easily steal the ball if it "slowly" crosses in front of the dribbler or if the bounce is too high. Also, the dribbler must shift the weight from one foot to the other during the cross-over to help protect the ball from the defense.

Table 3.6 summarizes the form, cues, and errors for the controlled, speed, and cross-over dribbles.

TABLE 3.6	Controlled, speed, and cross-over dribbles: Form, cues, and troubleshooting.			
TYPE OF DRIBBLE	**BIOMECHANICAL FORM & ACTION**	**VERBAL CUES**	**ERRORS***	**CAUSES OF ERRORS***
1. Controlled	■ Fingertips used ■ Hands cupped ■ Wrist flipped ■ Elbow kept close to body ■ Ball kept to side and slightly in front of body ■ Knees bent; crouched position ■ Ball protected with body ■ Knee-high dribbles ■ Head kept up	■ Use fingertips and flick wrist ■ Elbows in ■ Ball bounced to side and slightly in front of body ■ Bend knees ■ Bounce low ■ Head up	1. Ball stolen 2. Ball kicked by leg or hip of dribbler	1. Dribble too high; not protecting ball by putting body between ball and defender; ball bounced too far from body; cross-over too slow 2. Ball not dribbled to side and out in front of body
2. Speed	■ Fingertips used ■ Hands cupped ■ Wrist flipped ■ Ball bounced to side and more in front of body ■ Elbows, arms, and hands extended ■ Player runs to meet ball ■ Waist-high dribble ■ Head kept up	■ Use fingertips, flick wrist ■ Push ball out in front of body ■ Extend elbows ■ Bounce waist-high ■ Keep head up	3. Lose control of ball	3. Ball pushed too far in front
3. Cross-over	■ Fingertips used (on outside of ball) ■ Hands cupped ■ Wrists flicked ■ Low ball bounce in front of body ■ Close to body ■ Weight shifted to protect ball as it crosses over ■ Head kept up	■ Use fingertips ■ Flick outside ball in front ■ Keep ball close and low ■ Keep head up		

* Errors and Causes of Errors apply to each type of dribble.

◼ Dribble Drills

The following drills can be utilized to practice and learn the controlled dribble. The ball handler must learn to use either hand. Therefore, the off-hand should be stressed in each of these drills as well as the dominant hand.

Drill #14: Half Court On-Your-Own Drill

The Half Court On-Your-Own Drill (Figure 3.21) allows the ball handler the opportunity to concentrate on execution without being concerned with the defense. X_1's dribble to mid-court and back. They practice proper execution, speed, change of pace, and change of direction. Players should practice with both the dominant hand and the off-hand.

Drill #15 adds some defense-like resistance to practice of the controlled dribble.

CUES: 1. Use fingertips and flip wrist
2. Low bounce
3. Head up

Drill #15: Dribble Obstacle Drill

Three files are formed in the Dribble Obstacle Drill (Figure 3.22). Each file moves down court so the three are spaced equally between the endlines. The first players start dribbling down to the opposite end line, going by and around the players in their files. The defensive players are permitted to take one step in any direction in an attempt to steal the ball. The dribbler should practice control in working his/her way down the floor through the defense. When the dribbler gets by the last person in line, everyone moves up one position. X_2 now becomes X_1 and X_1 becomes the last player in the file. The drill continues in this manner.

CUES: 1. Keep ball low
2. Protect ball by keeping body between ball and defense
3. Head up

The Dribble Obstacle Drill also can be used to practice the cross-over dribble. The crossover should occur when the dribbler reaches each defensive player, and protection of the ball is vital. The ball handler should use either hand as appropriate.

Drill #16 : Keep-away Dribble

In the Keep-away Dribble Drill (Figure 3.23), the ball handler must concentrate on protecting the ball from the two defenders. This drill can be used as an application, self-test, or as a modified dribbling game.

CUES: 1. Keep head up
2. Use body and free hand to protect ball

Set up the half court into four quarters. Each quarter will have one dribbler (O) versus two defenders (X). O dribbles, avoiding X's attempts to steal or deflect the ball in the restricted area. If an

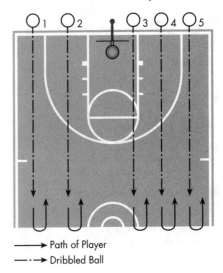

Figure 3.21
Half court on-your-own drill.

⟶ Path of Player
---⟶ Dribbled Ball

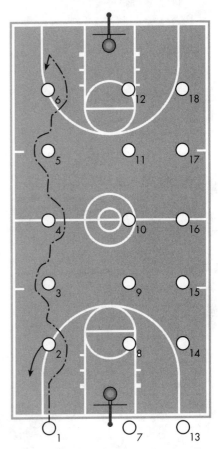

Figure 3.22
Dribble obstacle drill.

⟶ Path of Player
---⟶ Dribbled Ball

Figure 3.23

Keep-away dribble drill.

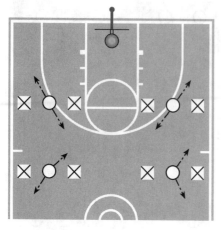

—·—▸ Dribbled ball

Figure 3.24

Speed race drill.

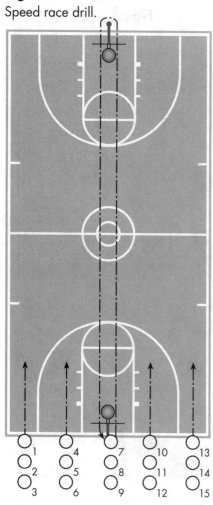

—·—▸ Dribbled Ball

X steals or deflects the ball, he/she becomes the dribbler and O goes on defense. Go for two to three minutes, then switch players.

Drills 17 through 19 are excellent for practicing the speed dribble. Drill 17 practices just the speed dribble, and Drill 18 adds the dimension of defensive pressure, and Drill 19 combines controlled and speed dribbling.

Drill #17: Speed Race Drill

For the Speed Race Drill, the players get into five lines of three (see Figure 3.24). The first person has the ball, and on the signal dribbles as fast as possible without losing control across the end line at the far end and back. Upon arriving at the starting point, the player should use a *flip pass* to give the ball to the second player in line. The first dribbler then goes to the end of the line. This drill should be practiced first using the dominant hand. As players' skill level progresses, the off-hand or alternate hands may be added to make this race more complex.

CUES: 1. Push ball out in front of the body
  2. Waist-high bounce
  3. Keep head up

Drill #18: Chase the Dribbler Drill

In Chase the Dribbler (Figure 3.25), the players are in pairs with the dribbler at half court and the chaser at the timeline. The dribbler (X_1) speed dribbles toward the basket and attempts a lay-up (see the discussion on shooting later in this section). The chaser (O_1) attempts to disrupt the dribbler's lay-up. This can be made into a game by awarding 2 points to the dribbler for making the lay-up. The chaser gets 1 point for a missed shot by the dribbler and an additional point if the chaser influences the miss without committing a foul. If the chaser commits a foul, 1 point is automatically awarded to the dribbler. X_1 then becomes the chaser and O_1 becomes the dribbler on the other side of the court.

CUES: 1. Keep head up
  2. Push ball in front of body
  3. Concentrate (shooter)

Figure 3.25 represents a right-handed dribble and lay-up. To practice a left-handed dribble and lay-up, the players will shift to the left side of the basket.

Drill #19: Control and Speed Dribble Combined Drill

The players line up in three lines of five (see Figure 3.26). They will use the control dribble with a change of pace and direction until they cross the center line (half court). Then they will speed dribble to the end line. After crossing the end line, they wait for all of the others before starting back. Each succeeding player starts as soon as the player in front of him/her gets out about 20 feet from the starting line.

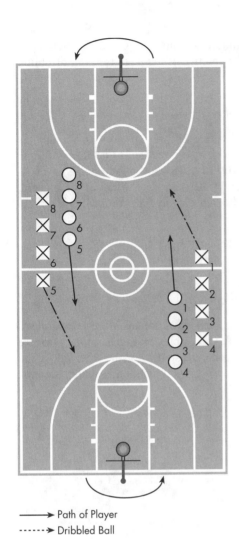

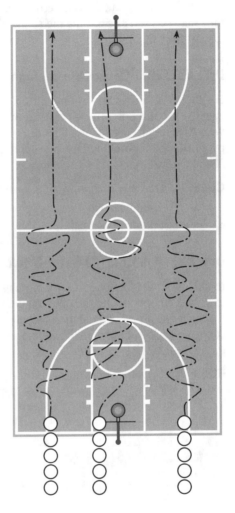

Path of Player
Dribbled Ball

Figure 3.25 (on left)
Chase the dribbler drill.

Figure 3.26 (on right)
Control and speed dribble combined drill.

CUES: 1. Head up

2. Ball low for controlled dribble

3. Ball waist-high for speed dribble

Drill #20: Cross-over and Pass Back Drill

The Cross-over and Pass Back (Figure 3.27) provides excellent practice. The players are divided into two groups and each group forms two lines facing its basket (see Figure 3.27). Players in each line have a ball. They dribble forward and use a cross-over dribble at the foul-circle area to proceed to the other side of the lane. They make a quick stop and pass to the first player in the opposite line from which they started, and then go to the end of the line. A chest pass, two-handed overhead pass, or one-handed push pass may be utilized for this drill. The receivers then follow the same procedure.

CUES: 1. Keep ball close to body and low

2. Quick wrist snap

3. Keep head up

Figure 3.27
Cross-over and pass back drill.

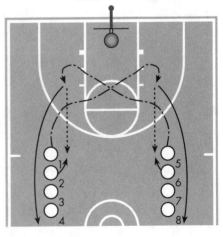

Path of Player
Passed Ball
Dribbled Ball

Drills 21, 22, and 23 can be used as modified games to practice dribbling, or they may be used to continue the sequential practice of the three types of dribbling discussed in this section.

Drill #21: Half Court One-on-One Dribble Drill

For the Half Court One-on-One Dribble (Figure 3.28), set up pairs of X's and O's equally at half court. Going in a counter-clockwise direction, O goes one-on-one with X in an effort to score. The dribbler (O) may use controlled, speed, or crossover dribbles or combinations of each to get by X (defender). After a shot is taken, X and O rotate lines and switch offense and defense. Only one group goes at a time.

CUES: 1. Use all dribbles when appropriate
2. Keep head up
3. Protect the ball

Drill #22: Full Court One-on-One Dribble Drill

In the Full Court One-on-One Dribble (Figure 3.29), pairs of players are set up, one of each pair on offense and the other on defense. O1 dribbles against X1 to the opposite baseline. The players should then switch positions and, starting on the other side of the court, go back to the original baseline. After one group reaches a baseline, the next group begins.

CUES: 1. Dribbler should not get caught on the sideline
2. Dribbling moves should be mixed

Figure 3.28 (on left)
Half court one-on-one dribble drill.

Figure 3.29 (on right)
Full court one-on-one dribble drill.

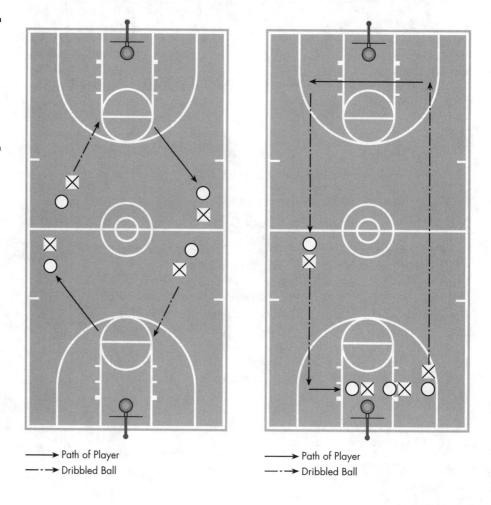

⟶ Path of Player
⟶ Path of Player
-·-▸ Dribbled Ball
-·-▸ Dribbled Ball

Drill #23: Dribble Tag Drill

Dribble Tag (Figure 3.30) is a drill in which each player is given a ball and sees how many of his/her teammates he/she can touch without losing control of the ball he/she is dribbling. The players must stay in the half-court area, and a teammate receives credit for a tag if he/she forces you to touch the center line or other out-of-bounds line. See who gets the most tags (touches). If you lose control of the ball, go outside the area and practice controlled, speed, and cross-over dribbles on your own until a new game begins.

CUES: 1. Keep head up
2. Keep ball low

Behind-the-Back Dribble

The final dribbling skill to be discussed is the **behind-the-back dribble.** This type of dribble is for players who will handle the ball primarily during team offensive play. The behind-the-back dribble can be used when a defensive player is overplaying the direction the dribbler is moving. This is a quick, fast action that takes on the following characteristics:

1. The ball is flicked close behind the back.
2. A quick flip with the dribbling hand sends the ball above the back of the knee and across the back of the thigh.
3. The ball then comes up under the opposite hand for continuation of the dribble.
4. The head stays up so the player can see the entire floor.

   Drills 15, 22, and 23 are good for practicing the behind-the-back dribble.

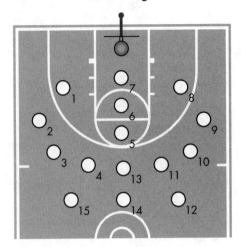

Figure 3.30
Dribble tag drill.

behind-the-back dribble
a dribble behind the back that the main ball handler uses during team offensive play when a defensive player is overplaying the direction of the dribbler

---

The individual offense body control fundamentals discussed in this section are:

- Body balance and style
- Pivoting
- Faking
- Cutting

Body balance is the basic basketball fundamental. Basketball requires quick starts and stops. Being able to move quickly in any direction and stop fast with good balance is vital to proper execution of all of the other basketball skills. The two-foot jump stop and the stride stop will be described in this section.

Pivoting is a maneuver of the feet to change the direction of the body while one foot keeps contact with the floor. Nearly all moves in basketball require a pivot. Players frequently pivot before taking a shot, while dribbling, in completing a rebound, and while playing defense. The front and reverse pivots will be the focus of pivoting.

Faking and *feinting* are tactics to make the opponent think the player is going to do one thing when he/she intends to do something entirely different. Body, eye, and ball fakes are included in this section.

Cutting is a quick movement by an offensive player without the ball, which is initiated to elude an opponent and enable the player to receive a pass in scoring position. Table 3.7 provides a summary of the body control fundamentals.

Body Control Fundamentals

body balance the ability to move quickly in any direction and stop fast with good balance

TABLE 3.7	Body control skills and uses.	
SKILL	**TYPES**	**USES**
Body balance	Basic working position	For most offensive plays with or without the ball
Stops	Two-foot jump stop	When a player is preparing to shoot or to gather his/her body for rebounding, etc.
	Stride stop	After completing a dribble or receiving a pass on the run
Pivots	Front	To change direction
		To gain position
	Reverse	To prepare for next move
Fakes	Body: head, shoulders, hips	To fake a shot or pass
	Eye	To set up the next move
	Ball	To direct the opponent
Screens	Lateral screen (screen-away)	To free a teammate from the defense
	Rear screen	

SKILL 4 Body Balance and Stops

The *basic working position* in basketball is one that has the following characteristics:

1. The weight is distributed equally on the balls of the feet.
2. The feet are in a toe-heel position about shoulder-width apart.
3. The knees are slightly flexed.
4. The body leans forward slightly.
5. The back is fairly straight with the head and eyes looking ahead to maximize one's peripheral vision.
6. The arms and hands are close to the body above the waist.
7. The fingers are spread and relaxed.

Stopping properly enables the player to prepare for the next movement or skill without losing balance and good body position. The drills included in this section might include fundamentals previously discussed. Therefore, many of the drills in this section feature combinations of skills.

Two-foot Jump Stop

two-foot jump stop *a stop used when defense is pressuring and an immediate pivot or turn is needed; also used to prepare for a lay-up or jump shot*

In executing the **two-foot jump stop,** the feet should hit the floor simultaneously with both feet parallel and entirely on the floor (Figure 3.31). The feet should be at least shoulder-width apart and the knees and hips slightly bent and relaxed to absorb the shock upon landing. The head and eyes always should be up.

pivot foot

Figure 3.31 (on left)
Foot placement for two-foot jump shot.

Figure 3.32 (on right)
Foot placement for stride stop.

This stop is used when a player is preparing to shoot a power lay-up or a jump shot. It also is the best stop when the defense is pressuring closely and an immediate pivot or turn is required after the stop.

Stride Stop

For the **stride stop,** the rear foot hits the floor first and becomes the pivot foot with the other foot following. One foot is in front of the other, in a stride position. The pivot foot should be the left foot for a right-handed player and the right foot for a left-handed player (see Figure 3.32).

stride stop *a stop in which the rear foot hits the floor first and becomes the pivot foot with the other foot following*

Balance and Stop Drills

The following drills allow for proper practice of the two-foot jump stop and the stride stop.

Drill #24: Start-and-Stop Drill

The front player in each file in the Start-and-Stop Drill (Figure 3.33) practices quick starts and stops down the floor and back. They may use either stop. Upon returning to their file, the players move to the rear and the next person goes. This drill can be practiced with the coach/teacher blowing a whistle to indicate when to stop or start, or it can be an on-your-own-drill. Also, the two-foot jump stop can be practiced by having each player dribble a ball and then picking it up and executing a proper two-foot jump stop on the coach/teacher whistle.

Drill #25: Change-Direction Drill

The Change-Direction Drill allows the players to practice starting and stopping while cutting at angles. Referring to Figure 3.34, O_1 and O_2 start the drill by running some 15 feet at a 45-degree angle. They make good stride stops, then change direction back about 15 feet at a 45-degree angle. O_3 and O_4 attempt to cut off O_1 and O_2's heels as they make their cut, stop, and change direction in an attempt to cut off the front player's heels again. This "dovetailing" continues down the court. The players in second position in each file start their cuts just as the first group starts the second cuts. When all players reach the other end of the court, the drill continues back in the same manner.

Figure 3.33 (on left)
Start-and-stop drill.

Figure 3.34 (on right)
Change-direction drill.

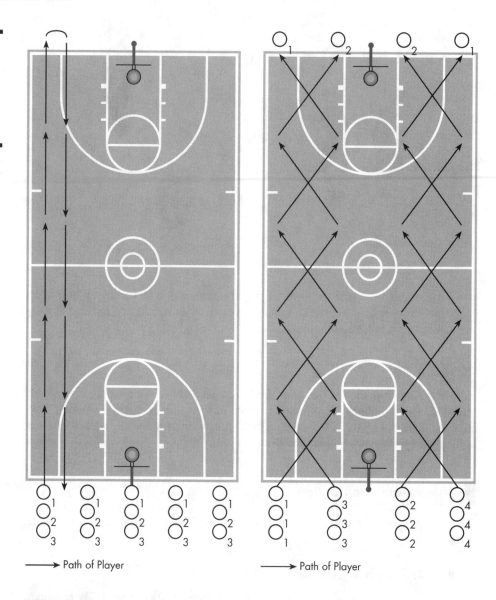

→ Path of Player   → Path of Player

SKILL 5 Pivoting

pivoting a maneuver of the feet to change the direction of the body while one foot keeps contact with the floor

Practically all moves in basketball require **pivoting.** Players often pivot at the end of a dribble, before taking a shot, after gaining possession of a rebound, and when positioning for defense. When pivoting, the following points should be considered.

1. Keep the ball close to the body, and keep the body between the ball and the defensive player.
2. Keep low with feet spread, knees bent, and head/eyes up.
3. Use either foot as the stationary or pivot foot.
4. Pivot to the outside in most cases.
5. Stop and pivot when driven toward the sideline or corner.

The two basic pivots are the front and the reverse. The main difference between the two is that the player swings his/her body toward the defender for the front pivot and swings it away for the reverse pivot.

Front Pivot

The front pivot is done as follows. When moving, the player executes the two-foot jump stop described earlier. If the player is making a *right-foot pivot,* he/she picks up his/her left foot, turns on the ball of right foot, swings the non-pivot leg (left) backward 180 degrees, and puts his/her left foot down. This will result in the player's back facing the direction he/she was going originally. In making a *left-foot pivot,* the player picks up his/her right foot and swings to his/her left. Figure 3.35 illustrates the front pivot.

Reverse Pivot

The reverse pivot (Figure 3.36) is used upon completing the stride stop when the ball must be protected from an aggressive defensive player. It also is used when a ball handler wants to reverse his/her direction and pass to a teammate who is trailing the ball. Here, the front foot crosses over quickly and the back is turned toward the defensive player.

Front and Reverse Pivot Drills

The following two drills can be utilized to practice the front and reverse pivots.

Drill #26: Front Pivot Floor-length Drill

For the Front Pivot Floor-length Drill (Figure 3.37) the players line up at one corner of the floor and the coach stands under the basket with a ball. The players start across the floor, each keeping about 10 feet in back of the one in front of him/her. They run toward the sideline with their eyes on the ball that the coach is holding. When they get near the sideline, they suddenly set the left foot when they are going to the right or the right foot when they are going to the left, and pivot toward the middle of the court. They then continue across the floor.

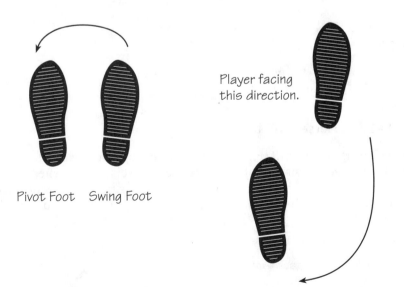

Pivot Foot   Swing Foot

Player facing this direction.

Figure 3.35 (on left)
Front pivot.

Figure 3.36 (on right)
Reverse pivot

Figure 3.37 (on left)
Front pivot floor-length drill.

Figure 3.38 (on right)
Reverse pivot drill.

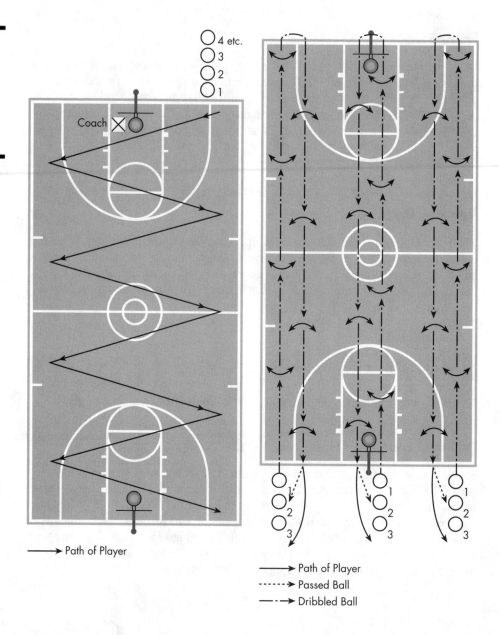

Coach

4 etc.
3
2
1

⟶ Path of Player

⟶ Path of Player
┈┈➤ Passed Ball
—·—➤ Dribbled Ball

CUES: 1. Jump stop
2. Stay low
3. Pivot to the outside

Drill #27: Reverse Pivot Drill

In the Reverse Pivot Drill (Figure 3.38), the front person in each file dribbles 15 to 20 feet, makes a stride stop, and executes a reverse pivot. After completing the reverse pivot, he/she pivots back to the original stride stop position and continues to dribble in the original direction, repeating the process down the floor and back.

CUES: 1. Stride stop
2. Pivot on back foot
3. Step with forward foot

SKILL 6 | Faking

One of the most important fundamentals in the game of basketball is **faking.** Although faking is often associated with offensive play, these moves are valuable to the defensive player as well. A good fake is followed by a quick move of some sort. Fakes can be made with or without the ball and are executed by the head, shoulder, body, and eyes in some combination. The type of fake used depends on the following things.

■ The player's position on the floor
■ Whether the player has the ball
■ The passing and shooting ability of the person with the ball (overall abilities)
■ The offensive or defensive situation
■ Where the ball is if one does not have it
■ Ability of the person guarding the player

The following are general guidelines for fake shots, fake passes, and fake cuts.

1. Make fakes sharp and distinct.
2. Protect the ball.
3. Don't fake unless you have a definite purpose in mind.
4. Determine your fakes by studying your opponent's moves.

CUES: Ball Fakes
1. Use to fake a shot dribble or pass
2. Use in combination with other body parts (such as head, eyes)

CUES: Body Fakes
1. Include head, shoulder, and/or hips
2. Use with or without the ball
3. Use before cutting past a defensive player
4. Use to change direction with or without the ball
5. Use before shooting

CUES: Eye Fakes
1. Use with or without the ball
2. Use before passing
3. Use while on defense

faking the ability to make an opponent commit himself/herself by making him/her think that the opposing player is going to do something different

SKILL 7 | Cutting

Cutting is an important asset to team offensive tactics. When cutting or moving quickly to elude a defender, a player should:

1. Know where the ball is.
2. Try to get the first step past the defender. The offensive player is going forward and the defender is moving backward or sideways.
3. Practice fast moves from standing, walking, or trotting positions.
4. Turn head toward the ball while making the cut.

Figures 3.39, 3.40, and 3.41 represent three types of cuts to free an offensive player from a defender.

cutting making quick moves to get into scoring position when an offensive player does not have the ball

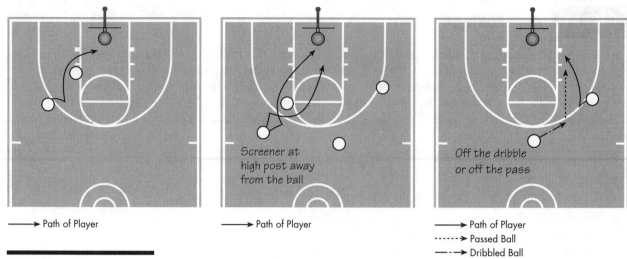

———▶ Path of Player · ———▶ Path of Player · ———▶ Path of Player
·········▶ Passed Ball
——·—▶ Dribbled Ball

Figure 3.39 (on left)
Change-of-direction cut.

Figure 3.40 (center)
Shuffle cut.

Figure 3.41 (on right)
Backdoor cut.

CUES: 1. Fake one way to go the other direction
2. Keep defender active and "watching" you

CUES: 1. Lead defender to screener
2. Change direction
3. Go to basket

CUES: 1. Set toward the ball
2. Cut behind screener and defender
3. Go to the basket

Shooting Fundamentals

The individual offense skills included in this section cover shooting fundamentals:

- Free throw fundamentals
- Jump shot fundamentals
- Lay-up fundamentals

Table 3.8 provides a summary of these shooting skills.

The *free throw* is an unguarded shot from the free throw line (15 feet from the basket) that is the result of a foul by the opponent. Although this is an unguarded shot and appears to be "easy" to do, many players have found it to be the most frustrating and difficult shot to execute. This might be explained in part by the importance the free throw often plays in the final outcome of many games. There are many different ways to shoot free throws. This section will examine the one-handed set shot as the main method. Players, however, should use the method in which they have the most confidence.

The *jump shot* is probably the most common and popular shot in basketball today. It originates from the one-handed push shot or set shot. In reality, it is virtually the one-handed set shot in the air. A good jump shooter can score consistently from a range of 20 feet from the basket. Scoring is the main objective in basketball, and jump shooting has become the primary scoring method.

The *lay-up* or lay-in is used when the player is close-in-around the basket. It has many variations, and players need to be able to make the lay-up while going toward the basket at different angles. Generally, a player is either dribbling (driving) to the basket when executing a lay-up or cutting to the basket in anticipation of the

TABLE 3.8	Shooting skills summary.	
SKILL	**TYPES**	**USES**
Free throw	One-handed set	To successfully execute unguarded free shot
Jump shot	One-handed	For distances up to 20 feet
Lay-up (Lay-in)	Regular	Coming at basket from right or left; along either baseline; or down middle of the court
	Baby hook (Jump hook)	To elude taller defenders; shot from 0–7 feet from basket

ball arriving in time to execute the lay-up. The two variations discussed here are the regular lay-up and the baby hook or jump hook.

Several general characteristics about shooting might be considered during the execution of any shot. The following shooting tips and hints will help most players get a higher percentage during game play.

1. Follow through on whatever type of shot is used.
2. Concentrate on the target before, during, and after the shot. Focus on either the front or back of the rim.
3. Keep the ball in position to pass, dribble, or shoot (triple threat position)—chest high and close to the body.
4. Shoot with confidence; know when to shoot.
5. Hold the ball loosely in the fingertips and avoid pressure by the thumb.
6. Practice from spots where you get the most shots.
7. When practicing shooting, get the ball away quickly and smoothly.
8. Learn the proper arc for each type of shot, and shoot softly.
9. Hold the ball between your eyes and the basket. Don't bring the ball over or in back of the head.
10. Learn to use the backboard, especially for close-in and angle shots.

SKILL 8 | Free Throws

The foul shot is a **free throw** at the basket from a line 15 feet away. This shot, taken without interference, is awarded to a player for an opponent's infringement of the rules. This shot is different from any other shot because the free throw shooter is not in a hurry, it is exactly the same distance each time, and the shot cannot be blocked. One would assume that a high percentage of those shots will be made because of the consistent conditions of this shot. Many games, however, have been decided based on the outcomes of free throw shooting and many of today's players are not considered good free throw shooters.

The two greatest hazards in free throw shooting seem to be poise and fatigue. Concentration and rhythm may be the most important factors in successful free throw shooting. Most coaches believe that free throws should be practiced so they become almost a reflex habit. The key is that every free shot, including preparation to shoot, must be the same each time. The following pointers or facts should be considered:

free throw an unhindered try for a goal from behind the free throw line awarded as a result of a foul by an opponent and valued at one point if scored; also called foul shot

1. Relax and take your time.
2. In preparing to shoot, take a deep breath, exhale, and then shoot.
3. Shoot to clear the leading edge of the rim.
4. Focus on the target (front or back edge of rim).
5. Hold the ball with the fingers in control.
6. At the start of each shot, always assume the same position of the feet, arms, hands, and fingers.
7. Practice to groove your shot.
8. Acquire a rhythm, and use the same rhythm on every shot.
9. Always use the hands and arms in the follow-through.

The one-handed push or set shot is the choice of most players in executing the free throw. It uses the same mechanics as the jump shot (discussed next) without the jump. Instead of jumping, the shooter rises up on his/her toes and returns to the same position that he/she was in to prepare for the shot. As an alternative, many coaches and teachers appreciate how effective the two-handed underhand shot has been over the years (and still is!). Though the mature player may not consider using this shot, its characteristic, soft back-spin has produced remarkable results.

The preparation phase of free throw shooting is critical to rhythm and concentration. The feet should be about shoulder-width apart. The weight should be forward toward the ball of the feet and the knees slightly flexed. The right foot might be slightly ahead of the left foot for a right-handed shooter and vice versa for a left-handed shooter.

The ball is held as if attempting the jump shot. The fingers and thumbs should be spread with palms almost facing each other when the ball is released. The shooting elbow is close to the body and directly under the ball. The ball is released by a quick extension of the elbows and a flick of the wrist and fingers of the shooting hand.

Sound fundamental shooting also requires use of the legs, as well as the arms and hands. The knees are slightly bent, and the head is up with the eyes focused on the target. The weight comes up high on the toes of the forward foot, along with an upward thrust from the rear foot. When the legs extend, the elbow is raised and the arm extension also begins. Thus, the shooter rises to his/her toes while extending the elbow and shooting arm. A complex follow-through allows for an extended shooting arm, a flexed wrist that has "fish-hooked," and extended knees and legs.

Poor free throw shooting is often the result of poor mechanics. The shooter should prepare for each shot the same way each time to maintain the rhythm of the shot. Relaxation and concentration are crucial to success. The ball should have a medium arc and backspin as it travels toward the basket.

Proper arm extension and flick of the wrist and fingers provide both components for the free throw. Many shooters try to shoot with only their arms and wrists without proper extension of their legs. This often is caused by fatigue, but when a shooter is tired, the legs become the critical component of the shot.

Figure 3.42 illustrates the pre-shot form for free throws. Table 3.9 summarizes the free throw fundamentals, teaching cues, possible errors and causes of errors.

Figure 3.42

Free throw position.

TABLE 3.9 Free throw shooting (one-handed push or set shot): Action, cues, and troubleshooting.

BIOMECHANICAL ACTION	VERBAL CUES	ERRORS	CAUSES OF ERRORS
■ Prepare to shoot the same each time	■ Rhythm and concentration are the keys	1. No arch; shot is short	1. Arm not fully extended; weak wrist and finger snap; legs not fully extended
■ Feet shoulder width apart	■ Right foot slightly ahead of left foot for right-handed shooter; feet shoulder-width apart		
■ Right foot slightly in front of left foot for right-handed shooter		2. Hurried shot	2. Preparation for the shot was not consistent; lack of concentration
■ Thumb and fingers spread on back and slightly under ball	■ Spread fingers and thumbs; keep elbow close to body under ball		
■ Non-shooting hand acts as guide	■ Focus on target (front or back of rim)	3. Shot off line	3. Arm not extended toward basket
■ Elbow close to body and under ball	■ Extend knees and legs to rise up on the toes		
■ Wrist and fingers snapped	■ Reach for the basket		
■ Shooting arm fully extended and reaching toward basket			
■ Knees and legs extended			
■ Rise up on the toes			

Free Throw Drills

Free throws must be practiced because so many games are decided by a team's ability to execute this shot. The best way to practice free throws is subject to debate. Some experts suggest shooting only two at a time, which simulates game conditions. Other experts suggest shooting again and again to establish a rhythm. The following drills use the two-shot theory.

Drill #28: Running Free Throw Drill

The players in the Running Free Throw Drill (Figure 3.43) are in groups of 3. First, player O₃ runs around the perimeter of the court while O₁ takes two free throws and O₂ rebounds. When O₃ returns, O₂ begins running the perimeter, O₃ shoots two free throws, and O₁ rebounds. This continues until each player has shot 20 free throws.

CUES: 1. *Relax before shooting*
2. *Concentrate*
3. *Extend legs, and rise up on toes*

Figure 3.43
Running free throw drill.

⟶ Path of Player

Figure 3.44
7-up drill.

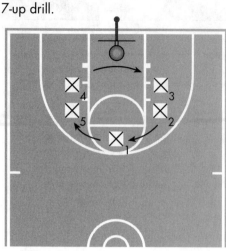

——▶ Path of Player

Drill #29: 7-Up Drill

The 7-Up (Figure 3.44) is a free throw shooting game. With five or six players at a basket, each player shoots one free throw. If X_1 makes his/her shot, the next shooter (X_2) must make his/her free throw or a point is assessed against him/her. If X_2 makes the free throw, X_3 must make his/her shot or 2 points will be assessed against him/her. Therefore, each shooter potentially can be assessed the same number of consecutive free throws made before his/her miss. If any player reaches 7 points, he/she must move to another basket and practice shooting two free throws a turn until a new game of 7-up is started.

CUES: 1. Take your time
2. Focus on the target
3. Extend legs and arms
4. Concentrate

| SKILL | 9 | Jump Shots |

jump shot *a shot similar in action to one-handed set shot but performed while shooter is in the air*

The **jump shot** has become the primary and basic shot used in the game of basketball. Through the years, many types of shots have been utilized and perfected. The set shot, two-handed or one-handed, the hook shot, the two-handed overhead, the knee-high push shot, the mechanical step-away, and the unlimited variety of close-in-around the basket shots have all proved to be useful depending upon the style of play or situation dictated during play. Any of these shots may be used today and some are utilized occasionally. Today's fast-paced and high-flying game, however, rarely allows for most of those shots. The jump shot, on the other hand, fits nicely into this style of play and has become the most important shot for today's players to master.

Fundamentals of the jump shot are basically the same as the one-handed set shot. The ball is held close to the chest and underneath the chin. The shooting hand is toward the back and slightly under the ball. The non-shooting hand is slightly toward the front and cupped. The non-shooting hand is used *only* for balancing the ball.

The fingers and thumb are spread on the shooting hand. The elbow of the shooting arm should be close to the body and directly under the ball. The hand, forearm, and elbow form a straight line up the body. The arm is in an "L" position.

A shooter must have good body balance. The shoulders should be squared-off and facing the basket, the feet shoulder-width apart, and the weight evenly distributed. The take-off is from the foot opposite the shooting hand. The player strives for height, not distance, while jumping straight up and coming straight down. Falling away or floating through the air makes the shot more difficult and often results in undesirable consequences (missed shot, charging foul, and so on).

The ball should be released quickly at the peak of, or just prior to, the jump but not after starting the descent. After a quick wrist and finger snap, the ball is released off the fingertips. The forefinger should finish pointing toward the target and the thumbs pointing down. This is the *follow-through phase* of the shot. Many coaches suggest that the shooter is reaching up and dropping the ball in the basket with a flip of the wrist or that the shooter is finishing the shot with the hand and wrist "fish-hooked."

The ball should be shot with arc, and the finger and wrist snap upon release should impart a backspin on the ball for a "soft touch." The shooter should be able to see the ball (using upward vision) at all times, and as the ball is released, the arm and elbow are fully extended. The non-shooting hand acts as a guide throughout and is released just before the wrist snap. Finally, the shooter must keep his/her eyes focused on the rim (front or back) from the time he/she decides to take a shot until the ball is well on the way to the basket.

From this description, it should be obvious that the jump shot is a complex and multifaceted skill with virtually all of the shooter's body parts involved in its execution. When introducing shooting to beginners, coaches and teachers should not expect the learner to remember every facet of the jump shot. Instead, they should teach one or two cues at a time in a progressive manner, to facilitate learning.

Because the jump shot is so complex, several things can go wrong. Missed shots may be the result of shooting while off-balance (floating or falling away) or not being squared-up with the basket. If the elbow is not under the ball and the wrist and fingers snap are not firm, the flight of the ball and the arc may be affected. Also, if the arm is not fully extended upon release, the ball often comes up short of the basket. Forcing shots is a common problem; the shooter has to adjust some component of the shot to get the ball past an aggressive defender. Rushing or hurrying the shot is almost always detrimental to success. Figure 3.45 shows the correct form for the jump shot, and Table 3.10 summarizes the actions, cues, errors, and causes of error of the jump shot.

The jump shot should be learned and practiced off the dribble and from a pass. The following jump shooting drills will give the player opportunities to do both. The drills are progressive in that they begin with the individual shooting without teammates or a defense, then teammates and defensive players are added to make the practice of jump shooting more gamelike.

Figure 3.45
Jump shot.

During jump shot:

- Release ball quickly at peak of jump
- Release ball off fingertips
- Shoot ball with an arc and use wrist snap to impart backspin
- Non-shooting hand acts as guide and is released just before wrist snap

Jump Shot Drills

Drill #30: Form Shooting Drill

In the Form Shooting Drill, the players are in three to five lines of three or four players, each with a ball. On signal, O's dribble and take a hard step and dribble, pushing off and thrusting into the air for a jump shot (see Figure 3.46). O's release their shot only a few feet above their head, exaggerating the form.

CUES: 1. Square-up shoulders
2. Jump straight up
3. Elbow under ball
4. Release ball off fingertips following wrist snap at height of jump

Figure 3.46

Form shooting drill.

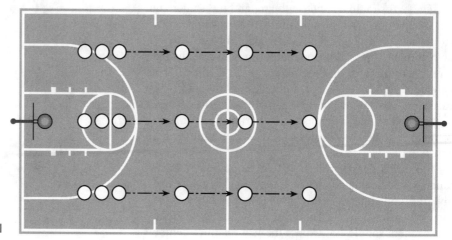

- - → Dribbled Ball

TABLE 3.10 | Jump shot: Action, cues, and troubleshooting.

BIOMECHANICAL ACTION	VERBAL CUES	ERRORS	CAUSES OF ERRORS
■ Ball is held toward back and slightly under the ball with shooting hand	■ Square-up shoulders to target	1. Shooting while off balance	1. Floating in air; fading away; not squaring shoulders
■ Non-shooting hand acts as guide toward front of ball	■ Jump straight up	2. Flight of ball off-line or shot is short	2. Elbow not under ball; taking eye off target; arm not extended toward basket
■ Fingers and thumb are spread on shooting hand	■ Elbow directly under ball	3. Forcing shots	3. Hurrying or rushing shot; shooting over aggressive defender who has position
■ Elbow is close to body and directly under the ball	■ Focus eyes on rim (front or back)		
■ Shoulders are squared facing the basket	■ Release ball off fingertips following wrist snap at height of jump	4. No arc or backspin	4. No follow-through; weak wrist and finger snap
■ Feet shoulder-width apart and weight distributed evenly before jump			
■ Take-off is from opposite foot of shooting hand			
■ Player jumps up straight			
■ Ball is held above eyes			
■ Ball released at peak of jump			
■ Wrist and fingers snapped with forefinger of shooting hand pointing toward basket with thumbs down			
■ Shooting arm fully extended while reaching toward basket			

Drill #31: Mini Jump Shot Drill

For the Mini Jump Shot Drill (Figure 3.47), mark spots 1–5 on the court. O takes jump shots starting from point 1, then 2 through 5. O then goes back from spots 5 to 1 and repeats spots 1 to 5 for a total of 15 shots. *Variation:* A defensive player stands in front of each spot with hands up.

CUES: 1. Square-up shoulders
            2. Jump straight up
            3. Focus eyes on rim (front or back)

Drill #32: Two-ball Jump Shot Drill

For the Two-ball Jump Shot Drill (Figure 3.48), O_3 sets up on the foul line right elbow. O_1 and O_2 each have a basketball. On signal, O_1 passes to O_3, who takes a jump shot. O_3 then slides to the left elbow for a pass from O_2 and takes a jump shot. O_3 repeats this movement, sliding back and forth for one minute. O_1 and O_2 rebound shots. *Variation:* Do this drill from wing and corner positions A and B.

CUES: 1. Square-up shoulders
            2. Jump up - no floating

Drill #33: Quick-shot Drill

The Quick-shot Drill has three people at a basket and uses two basketballs. The three positions are shooter, passer, and rebounder. Each player has 55 seconds to shoot from each of the three spots (right, left, and the free throw line). The players have 5 seconds to rotate to a new position after the time is up. The shooter goes to the rebounding position. The rebounder becomes the passer and the passer becomes the shooter. After all three shoot from the position, they change to another spot and continue the routine. The rebounder counts the number of baskets made, and the passer counts the number of shots attempted. Each shooter's percentage can be recorded. Each player should get off about 22 to 25 shots every 55 seconds. Players are not allowed to dribble; they should catch and shoot in one motion. Figures 3.49, 3.50, and 3.51 show the three main positions for this drill.

→ Path of Player

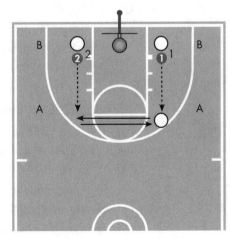

→ Path of Player
┈┈▶ Path of Ball

Figure 3.47 (on left)
Mini jump shot drill.

Figure 3.48 (on right)
Two-ball jump shot drill.

Figure 3.49

Quick-shot drill: position 1.

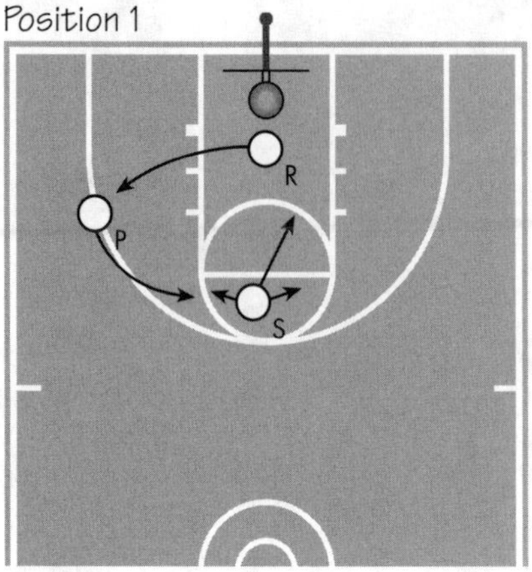

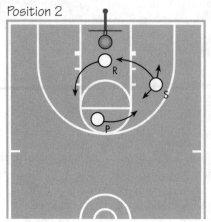

Position 1

Figure 3.50

Quick-shot drill: position 2.

Position 2

Figure 3.51

Quick-shot drill: position 3.

Position 3

P = Passer   R = Rebounder   ——▶ Path of Player
S = Shooter

CUES: 1. Hands up to receive pass
2. Square up, release ball quickly
3. Jump up

Figure 3.52

Chair placement and action for speed shooting drill.

——▶ Path of Player   ■ Chair
—·—▶ Dribbled Ball

Drills 30–33 worked either on form shooting or shooting after receiving a pass. The next set of drills provide practice for the jump shot off the dribble.

Drill #34: Speed Shooting Drill

To set up the Speed Shooting Drill, place three chairs on the court as shown in Figure 3.52. The player starts behind the middle chair. He/she dribbles with his/her outside hand from the middle chair to a side chair, squares to the basket, and shoots the jump shot. After shooting the ball, he/she rebounds the shot, dribbles out around the middle chair with the opposite hand, and goes to the other side chair, where he/she executes a jump shot. The player continues to move from one side to the other. The drill lasts one minute.

CUES: 1. Use outside hand for dribble
2. Square up
3. Jump straight up
4. Follow through

Drill #35: 25-Shot Drill

In the 25-Shot Drill (Figure 3.53), Player 1 moves from side to side; Player 2 is the rebounder and the passer. Player 1 will take 25 shots following this formula:

10 no-dribble jump shots
5 one-dribble jump shots
5 more than one dribble jump shot
5 anything goes (e.g., 2 dribbles to the right, spin dribble left, and then a jump shot)

Player 1 must move constantly and as if he/she were in a game.

CUES: 1. Jump straight up
      2. Release ball at peak of jump
      3. Follow through

Drill #36: Jump Shot Shooting Drill

Four players are situated on each court in this Jump Shot Shooting Drill (see Figure 3.54). This drill utilizes both baskets. The remainder of the squad lines up off the court awaiting the next game. Each of the players in the game has a ball. The objective of the game is to make 15 jump shots before the other three players in the foursome. Each player must call aloud his/her score and retrieve his/her own shot. The game starts on the coach's whistle. When a player in the foursome hits 15 shots, the game is over. The winner stays on the court, and the waiting players take their turn, making up the shooting foursome.

CUES: 1. Keep head up (dribble)
      2. Square up
      3. Release ball at peak of jump
      4. Follow shot

Drill #37: Dribble and Shoot Drill

As illustrated in Figure 3.55, the steps in the Dribble and Shoot Drill are:

1. The squad is divided into two teams.
2. Each line will dribble to half court right-handed, cross the ball behind the back and dribble left-handed to the top of the key. Each player will shoot a jump shot at this point. If he/she misses, he/she rebounds and comes back to shoot until he/she makes the jumper. After making the shot, he/she must make a foul shot.
3. As soon as the player makes the foul shot, he/she returns to the other end, repeating the same routine as previously described (right/left dribble, jumper, and foul shot). He/she then passes the ball to the next player in line.

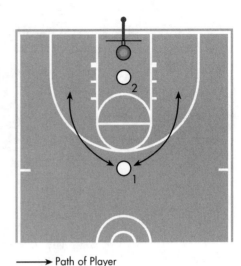

Figure 3.53
25-shot drill.

⟶ Path of Player

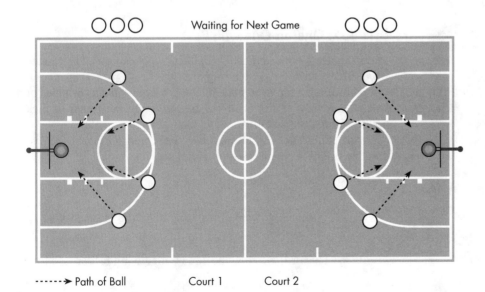

Figure 3.54
Jump shot shooting drill.

- - - - - ➤ Path of Ball   Court 1   Court 2

Figure 3.55

Dribble and shoot drill.

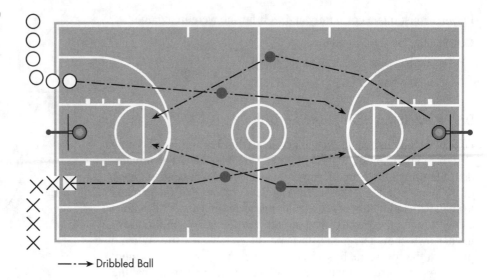

—·—▶ Dribbled Ball

The first team to finish is the winner.

CUES: 1. Keep head up

2. Focus eyes on rim

3. Don't rush

The next set of jump shooting drills is designed to be more gamelike. The drills include elements of passing, receiving, screening, faking, dribbling, and shooting, in addition to defensive pressure.

Drill #38: Pick and Jump Shot

To execute the Pick and Jump Shot Drill (Figure 3.56), X defends O_1 on top of the circle. O_2 and O_3 stand still at each elbow one stride away from the lane. O_1 goes either to the right or to the left and sets up his/her dribble to utilize the pick. O_1 takes a jump shot and O_1 strides past the pick of O_2 or O_3.

CUES: 1. Set up dribble

2. Square up

3. Release ball at peak of jump

Figure 3.56

Pick and jump shot drill.

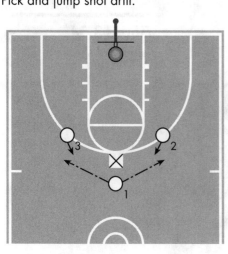

——▶ Path of Player

—·—▶ Dribbled Ball

Drill #39: One-on-One with Post

In the One-on-One with Post Drill, the players pair up and alternate from offense to defense each time they work.

The offensive player may try to get away on the dribble, or he/she may pass to the post, but he/she is not permitted to pick his/her defensive player off on the post.

Two cones (■) can be placed as indicated on Figure 3.57 to give the offense some help as potential screens.

CUES: 1. Protect the ball with body

2. Use shuffle cut

3. If shooting from pass, jump straight up quickly

4. Off dribble, keep head up

Variation: This drill also may be done with a wing feeder (see Figure 3.58).

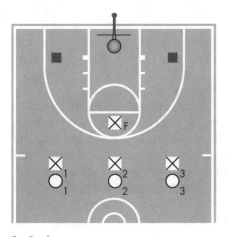

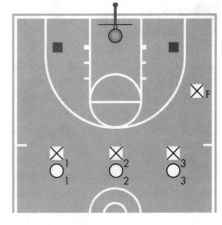

F = Feeder

F = Feeder

Figure 3.57 (on left)
One-on-one drill with post.

Figure 3.58 (on right)
One-on-one drill with wing.

Drill #40: Two-on-Two with Post

In the Two-on-Two with Post Drill, the players line up as in pairs in their normal position with one pair on defense, one pair on offense, and the third pair ready to move in on the next turn. The offense becomes the next defense, the waiting pair becomes the next offense, and the defense waits out a turn. The post player may be used as an outlet and a feeder. Figure 3.59 illustrates this drill.

Variation: This drill may be done with a wing feeder (see Figure 3.60).

CUES: 1. Maintain 15 foot spacing
2. Use shuffle cut
3. Keep head up

Drill #41: Three-on-Three Continuity Drill

The Three-on-Three Continuity Drill (Figure 3.61) begins with the coach passing the ball to O3. O1 makes a cut off O2's screen, either baseline or over the top. O2 holds the screen and then drifts out to replace O1. O3 looks for O1 inside or goes one-on-one with his/her player, X3. If O3 does neither, he/she passes back to the coach, who reverses the ball to O2. Now O3 comes off O1's screen, and the continuity begins.

CUES: 1. Set firm screen
2. Use shuffle cuts
3. Keep head up
4. Square up on jump shot

Figure 3.59
Two-on-two drill with post.

Figure 3.60
Two-on-two drill with wing.

Figure 3.61
Three-on-three continuity drill.

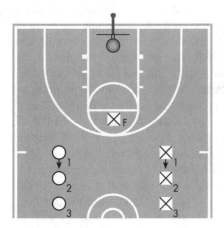

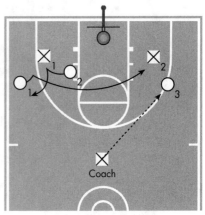

F = Feeder

F = Feeder

⟶ Path of Player
------⟶ Path of Ball

SKILL 10 | Lay-ups

lay-up a shot taken near the basket usually by playing the ball off the backboard; also called lay-in

baby hook or jump hook a shot taken with one hand in a sweeping motion over the top of a tall defender

The **lay-up** shot is used close to the basket, and the goal of most offenses and players is to get an uncontested lay-up shot. If this is possible, the regular or orthodox lay-up (Figure 3.62) is appropriate. In today's game, uncontested lay-ups usually are the result of good defensive play that results in stealing the ball from the opponent, followed by a break-away lay-up. Getting an uncontested lay-up within the framework of a set offense is much more difficult. Defenses go to great lengths to deny clear access to the basket. Therefore, most shots have to be taken over towering defensive players. The **baby hook** or **jump hook** is a type of lay-up shot that can be taken a few feet from the basket and can be projected over big players in a way that still allows for a "soft" laid up shot.

Three phases or steps are involved in the lay-up:

1. The approach
2. The take-off
3. The lay-up

In the *approach,* the player dribbles toward the basket or cuts to receive a pass as it arrives at the basket. The approach is important because the player is preparing for the take-off. The player wants to plant his/her opposite foot from the shooting hand. For this to happen, the player has to see where he/she is in relation to the basket. To arrive at the proper take-off position, the shooter may have to adjust his/her stride on the dribble or cut.

The player executes the *take-off* by pushing or jumping off the foot opposite the one that is planted at the end of the approach, from the selected shooting hand. As the take-off foot slaps the floor, the shooter begins to gather himself/herself. This involves catching the ball from the fast dribble or receiving the pass. The ball is brought up by the face, protected by both hands. Also, the shooter should focus the eyes on a spot on the backboard above the rim toward the shooter's side. The shooter must jump up (vertically) toward the backboard, not out toward the end line. This upward lift is aided by the free knee swinging ahead of the take-off leg. The upward lift of the body allows the player to place the ball on the backboard. A broad-jump (horizontal) style of take-off often makes the lay-up difficult, resulting in many errors.

The player completes the *lay-up* step or phase upon reaching the peak of the jump. At this point, the body is in a set position for the shot. The shooting hand takes over control of the ball. This hand is on the side of the ball. As the shooting arm is extended toward the backboard, the ball is released at the peak of the jump. The ball should be placed high and softly on the board as it rolls off the fingertips following a quick upward flip of the wrist. When the player descends to the floor, he/she will land in a position near the basket.

Critical points in successfully executing the lay-up are to jump up, not out, and to release the ball at the peak of the jump. Broad jumping, or jumping out toward the baseline, is a common mistake. This type of jump makes it harder to control the body and won't allow for the height needed to release the ball softly to the backboard and basket.

Figure 3.62

Regular (orthodox) lay-up.

For lay-up:

- Keep eyes on target
- Raise non-shooting hand for balance
- Use non-shooting foot as takeoff foot
- Release ball at peak of jump
- Use backboard whenever possible

Jumping off the wrong foot is another common problem. This is often the result of a lack of practice in shooting the lay-up from different angles and the player's lack of confidence in using either hand for shooting.

Pushing the ball too hard off the board causes many missed lay-ups. The ball has to be placed softly against the backboard, and flipping the wrist upward and rolling the ball off the fingers enhances the gentle motion. Many lay-ups are missed because the shooter does not keep his/her eye focused on the target throughout the three phases of the lay-up. Dropping or turning the head before the shot is completed often causes the ball to be shot short or too hard, resulting in missed opportunities. Table 3.11 summarizes the cues and errors associated with the regular lay-up.

TABLE 3.11 Regular lay-up: Action, cues, and troubleshooting.

BIOMECHANICAL ACTION	VERBAL CUES	ERRORS	CAUSES OF ERRORS
Approach Phase: ■ Adjusting stride while dribbling or cutting toward the basket ■ Planting opposite foot from shooting hand	■ Adjust stride during approach ■ Plant opposite foot from shooting hand	1. Jumping out (broad jumping), not up 2. Jumping off the wrong foot	1. No stride adjustment; not getting body under control to lift upward 2. Lack of practice; lack of confidence
Take-Off Phase: ■ Gathering ball with both hands and bringing ball to face ■ Focusing eyes on target ■ Pushing off plant foot ■ Swinging free knee ahead of take-off leg ■ Jumping upward	■ Gather ball and jump upward off take-off foot ■ Focus eyes on target ■ Release ball with upward wrist flip at peak of jump ■ Use backboard whenever possible	3. Ball thrown against backboard 4. Eye not on target	3. Arm not fully extended; excessive spin placed on ball; body floating out 4. Shooter didn't focus on target during approach; shooter worried about defender; shooter jumping out, not up
Lay-up Phase: ■ Body is under control in vertical jump ■ Shooting hand takes control on side of ball ■ Shooting arm is extended ■ Ball is released with a quick upward flip of wrist ■ Ball rolls off of fingers at peak of jump ■ Ball hits softly against backboard ■ Shooter lands near the basket			

For beginners, the lay-up can be a difficult shot to learn. Initial drills may require the player to break down the shot into small, segmented parts and then, as the player becomes comfortable with each part, put together the segments. The following discussion examines possible ways to break down the lay-up.

1. *One step and shoot.* The player takes one step (left foot for a right-handed shooter, right foot for a left-handed shooter) and shoots. This will help the player develop a feel for the opposition of the arms and legs required to execute the lay-up. This is the *take-off phase* of lay-up shots.

   In this segment, the player should concentrate on pushing off the foot that is taking the step and lifting the other leg (right for right-handed shooter).

2. *Two steps and shoot.* The player takes a step with the right foot, then with left (right-handed shooter) and shoots. Here, the shooter should concentrate on the *lay-up phase* or extending the arm toward the backboard as the player leaves the floor from the take-off.

3. *Two dribbles with the two steps.* This allows the shooter to practice the approach phase of the shot and combine the take-off and lay-up phases.

The shooter should concentrate on catching the ball from the second dribble, pushing off the opposite foot from the shooting hand (second step), and extending the arms toward the backboard as the player's body leaves the ground.

More steps and dribbles can be added as the player grows more comfortable.

Lay-up Drills

The following drills are designed for players who have some comfort with executing the lay-up. Players must be able to make lay-up shots while driving or cutting to the basket from different angles. Practice drills should come from both the left and the right sides of the basket, along either baseline, and down the middle of the court.

Figure 3.63

Dribble drives from side drill.

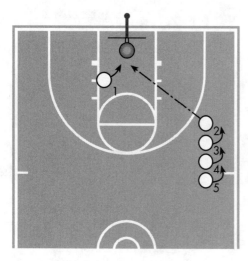

⟶ Path of Player

—·⟶ Dribbled Ball

Drill #42: Dribble Drives from Side Drill

For the Dribble Drives from Side Drill, the players line up with five at a basket, as indicated in Figure 3.63. The person underneath rebounds the ball, passes out, and goes to the end of the line. The shooter stays underneath to rebound for the next driver. This drill should be done on both sides of the lane. The shooter also can go all the way under for the baby hook.

CUES: 1. Adjust stride
2. Focus eyes on target (not ball)
3. Push off opposite foot
4. Reach for backboard

Drill #43: One-Minute Lay-up Drill

In the One-Minute Lay-up Drill (Figure 3.64), O_1 lines up on the right side of the foul line. On the signal, O_1 dribbles toward the basket, does a right-handed lay-up, rebounds, dribbles back to the foul line, and repeats the process for 20 seconds. On the signal, O_2 goes to the left side of the lane and repeats the same movement with a left-handed dribble and lay-up for 20 seconds. Finally, on the signal, O_3 goes from the middle of the lane, using either hand,

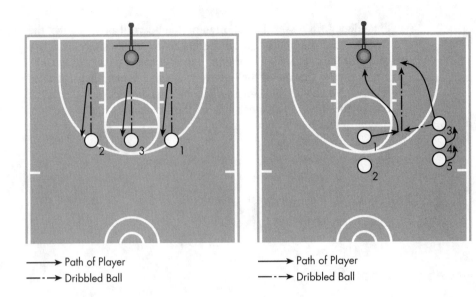

Figure 3.64 (on left)
One-minute lay-up drill.

Figure 3.65 (on right)
Under basket from the move drill.

for 20 seconds. This drill can be used as a self-test, counting the total number of baskets made during the minute.

CUES: 1. Push off opposite foot
2. Focus eyes on target
3. Reach for backboard

When driving down the middle of the lane, a player may lay the ball over the front of the rim using either hand or may choose to veer to the right or to the left to utilize the backboard.

Drill #44: Under Basket from the Move Drill

In the Under Basket from the Move Drill, the players line up with five at a basket as indicated in Figure 3.65. The side player passes to the player on the post and cuts for a return pass for the shot. The shooter and passer retrieve the ball before it can touch the floor, pass it back to the sideline, and exchange lines. After a player has worked in both positions, he/she goes to the opposite side of the floor so the drill can continue back and forth from one side to the other.

The types of shots practiced from each side of the floor in this drill are:

1. Quick lay-up after a head fake to the inside
2. Quick stop and fade-away from a few feet out
3. All the way under for a hook

CUES: 1. Keep head up for return pass
2. Adjust stride
3. Plant opposite foot
4. Jump upward

Drill #45: Long Pass from the Board Drill

The Long Pass from the Board Drill combines the baseball pass (discussed earlier), rebounding, the lay-up, and speed dribbling. Therefore, it allows several fundamental skills to be practiced.

The players line up as indicated in Figure 3.66, with 8, 9, and 10 each having a ball and 1 lined up on the side approximately one step farther out than the foul line

Figure 3.66

Long pass from the board drill.

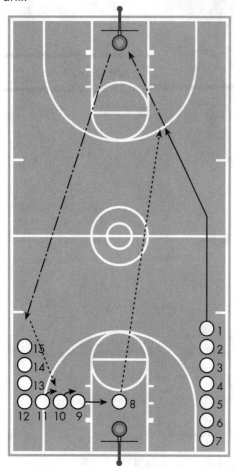

→ Path of Player

----→ Passed Ball

—·→ Dribbled Ball

extended. As 8 tosses the ball high on the board, 1 breaks down the sideline and then cuts toward the basket when he/she gets a few feet past the center line. Then 8 tries to complete a baseball pass to 1 and goes to the end of the line from which 1 broke, then 1 tries to receive the pass, score, retrieve the ball, and speed-dribble to the end of the line on the other side of the floor, and pass to the first player in that line without a ball.

CUES: 1. Catch ball

2. Adjust stride

3. Focus eyes on target

4. Jump up

Hook Shot

Drill 44, Under Basket from the Move drill, and the following drills provide opportunities to use the baby or jump hook.

The baby hook or jump hook can be utilized to lay the ball over the top of tall, aggressive defenders. For this shot, the ball is held away from the defender with one hand and released so it hits high on the backboard. The non-shooting hand is raised to protect the shot. Again, the shooter plants the foot opposite the shooting hand and pushes upward. The ball is released at the peak of the jump, and the wrist is flipped forward and up so the ball rolls softly off the fingers. The ball is banked off the backboard with a soft touch for more accuracy. The eyes must be on the target throughout the shot. (Table 3.10 included possible errors and causes of errors for the baby hook.)

Players must be able to make lay-up shots while driving or cutting to the basket from different angles. Practice drills should come from both the left and the right sides of the basket, along either baseline and down the middle of the court.

The next two drills combine jump and hook shooting with lay-ups. These drills may be used as self-test activities or modified games in practicing shooting.

Drill #46: 5-3-1 Shooting Drill

The 5-3-1 Shooting Drill (Figure 3.67) utilizes all baskets, and players work in pairs. O takes three shots starting at the foul line:

1. Foul line jump shot   =   5 points
2. Anywhere from 10 feet   =   3 points
3. Lay-up   =   1 point

This movement is repeated for one minute. The player with the highest total is the winner.

Variation: Give a pump fake and one dribble before taking the shot.

CUES: 1. Follow shot

2. Focus on target

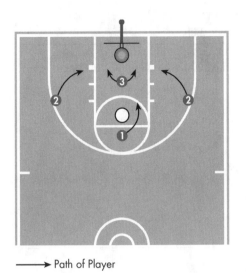 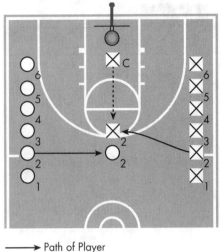

→ Path of Player

→ Path of Player
----→ Path of Ball

Figure 3.67 (on left)
5-3-1 shooting drill.

Figure 3.68 (on right)
Number one on one drill.

Drill #47: Number One on One Drill

For the Number One on One Drill, two teams are set up on the sideline with consecutive numbers on each team (see Figure 3.68). C rolls the ball past the top of the circle and calls out a number. The same number from each team comes out. The player who secures the ball first is on offense and the other player is on defense. The players go one-on-one until one of them scores a basket.

CUES: 1. Square shoulders
2. Pump fake
3. Focus eyes on target

The transition skills included in this section involve gaining control of the ball:

- Defensive rebounding
- Offensive rebounding
- Loose balls
- Fast breaks

In *defensive rebounding,* a team takes possession of the ball following an opponent's missed shot and can begin to concentrate on offensive play at the other end of the court. Usually, more shots are missed than made during a basketball game at all levels of play. Therefore, the defensive team must strive to allow the offensive team only one chance to score per trip.

Offensive rebounding gives the team that just attempted to score another chance at scoring, and perhaps an advantage over their opponents. A second chance often means a score that more than half the time would have been a missed opportunity.

Defensive and offensive rebounding are considered transitional skills in this section because upon gaining possession of the ball, both teams must quickly make some significant change from what they were just doing to something quite different. A team may have been playing defense and now, with possession of the ball (defensive rebound), one of its players is fast breaking to its offensive **basket** in an attempt to get an easy score or an advantage over the opponent. Or a team may have just missed a shot but, by getting to the ball first (offensive rebound) may get an easy tip-in or another chance to set up the offense for an extra try at

TRANSITION SKILLS

Gaining Possession of the Ball

basket *the goal*

TABLE 3.12 Gaining possession of the ball skills.

SKILL	TYPES	USES
Rebounding	Defensive	To take ball away from opponent To initiate fast break To begin offensive play
	Offensive	To get second chance to score
Loose Balls	Deflected passes Errant passes Blocked shots Mishandled offensive skills	To obtain an advantage over opponent

scoring. In either case, the rebound has resulted in both teams making a quick adjustment or transition into some new action.

If there is a *loose ball,* one team may get an advantage over the other by gaining possession. Both teams begin to make the transition from one perspective to another.

Transitioning has changed the nature of the game of basketball throughout its evolution and makes the game exciting to play and watch. Table 3.12 provides a summary of the skills involved in gaining possession of the ball.

SKILL 11 Rebounding

Rebounding in basketball is a matter of individual effort, determination, anticipation, and hard work. While basketball is a complete, team-oriented game in all phases, rebounding usually comes down to aggressive play. The player who is most determined to get the ball is more than likely the one who will get it. The player who has the best position on the court also is likely to get the ball. Some tips about rebounding are as follows.

1. Assume that every shot will be missed.
2. Have hands up ready to respond to the ball.
3. Do not get caught too far under the basket.
4. Upon gaining possession of the ball, protect it with the body and elbows.
5. Get the ball away from the basket quickly and safely.
6. Avoid passing across the opponent's basket. Also, most missed shots bounce toward the side of the court opposite from where the shot was taken, and the pass-out almost always should be in the same direction as that from which the rebound is coming.
7. Don't dribble too much after a rebound; dribble to clear from the defense, but pass as soon as possible.
8. Expect contact, and maintain poise.

defensive rebounding
the act of gaining possession of the ball by the defensive team after the offensive team has attempted and missed a field goal

Defensive Rebounding

Defensive rebounding is crucial to good basketball because in most games more shots are missed than made. Therefore, the defensive team has to make sure that the offensive team gets only one chance to score per trip. Gaining possession of the ball prevents the opponent from scoring points and often translates into one team controlling the tempo of a game.

The fundamentals of defensive rebounding begin with the assumption that every shot taken will be missed. When the shot goes up, the defender's arms and fingers should be up, pointing to the ceiling. Next, each defensive player should block his/her offensive counterpart off the boards by using either a front pivot or a reverse pivot. In this **blocking off,** the defensive player gets the inside position on the offensive player (Figure 3.69). The defender uses his/her body to get between the offensive player and the ball (basket). When the defender gets into position, he/she should step into the offensive player, taking up the distance between the two. No room is left for the offensive player to maneuver (Figure 3.70). Finally, release quickly and aggressively go after the ball.

Thus, the process of defensive rebounding is:

1. When a shot is taken, the defender pivots in front of the opponent and raises the hands above the shoulders, with the elbows out.
2. Once the opponent is blocked out, the defender goes for the ball (Figure 3.71).
3. When the defender has gained control of the ball, the legs are spread, knees bent, and the ball is protected with body, arms, and legs. The elbows should be out but not swinging from side to side, which may cause the rebounder to be assessed a foul (Figure 3.72).
4. Immediately, he/she looks for an outlet pass or quickly dribbles clear from the (new) defense to be able to complete a pass.

The rebounder should be sure that he/she is not pushed under the basket and out of position. Also, the rebounder should know the probable rebounding angle of the ball. Not understanding where the ball will ultimately go is an error that can cost teams a game.

Offensive Rebounding

Offensive rebounding often results in easy or "cheap" points because the defense usually is out of position. Also, many offensive rebounds end in a two-shot free throw opportunity and, again, a chance to score when it appeared that the offense had misfired.

blocking off the positioning of a defensive player in such a manner as to prevent an offensive player from going to the basket for a rebound

offensive rebounding the act of gaining possession of the ball by the offensive team after a missed field goal attempt by the rebounder or a teammate

Figure 3.69 (on left)
Blocking off.

Figure 3.70 (on right)
Blocking off.

Figure 3.71 (on left)
Defensive rebounding.

Figure 3.72 (on right)
Defensive rebounding.

tipping *a quick, one-handed flip of a missed field goal try that results in a score*

The fundamentals of offensive rebounding are similar to the basics of defensive rebounding. The situation is different in most cases, however, because the offensive player is often behind the defender. Therefore, the offensive player must be active. Constant moving may open a rebounding lane for the player or a teammate. Also, this movement makes it more difficult for the defender to block him/her out.

Offensive players should watch the flight of the ball and anticipate the rebounding angle of the ball. This anticipation plus movement can give the offensive player an edge or extra step over the defense.

An offensive player should try to get a hand on every missed shot. The offensive rebounder should play through the ball and try to get contact just prior to reaching the peak of his/her jump and just before the complete extension of his/her elbow and wrist.

Offensive rebounders should use their wrists and fingers for **tipping.** The idea is to keep the ball alive so they or a teammate can control the ball for a score or for a "second" possession.

Though offensive rebounders might try to force the defensive players under the basket and out of position, it is a mistake to foul unnecessarily by going over the defender's back. Shoving or pushing the defender will result in a foul on the offense; therefore, offensive rebounders should keep their hands up and jump up, not over, their opponents.

Table 3.13 summarizes the cues and errors for rebounding.

Rebounding Drills

To practice rebounding, blocking off should be stressed for defensive rebounding, and moving and tipping for offensive rebounding. One-on-one, two-on-two, three-on-three, and five-on-five situations should be utilized. The following drills will help improve defensive rebounding.

TABLE 3.13	Rebounding: Action, cues, and troubleshooting.			
TYPE OF REBOUNDS	**BIOMECHANICAL ACTION**	**VERBAL CUES**	**ERRORS**	**CAUSES OF ERRORS**
Defensive	■ Raise arms and point fingers to ceiling ■ Use front or reverse pivot to get body between offensive player and basket (ball) ■ Step into offensive player to take up room ■ Anticipate angle of rebound, and release quickly ■ Grab ball with two hands and bring into chest ■ Elbows out, legs spread, knees bent ■ Outlet pass or clear defense	■ Raise arm and point fingertips up ■ Block off ■ Anticipate angle of rebound ■ Catch with both hands at peak of jump ■ Protect ball	1. Not blocking off offensive player 2. Getting caught under basket 3. Not anticipating angle of rebound	1. Losing sight or feel of offensive player 2. Allowing offense to force or push out of position 3. Not watching flight of ball
Offensive	■ Be active—move ■ Anticipate angle of rebound ■ Raise arms; get hand on ball ■ Tip ball with wrist and finger snap; back up on backboard ■ Grab ball with two hands, if possible ■ Bring ball to chest, elbows out	■ Be active—move ■ Raise arms ■ Tip ball ■ Protect ball	1. Going over defender's back 2. Not anticipating angle of rebound	1. Not jumping up 2. Not watching flight of ball

Drill #48: Timing Across the Board Drill

To begin the Timing Across the Board Drill (Figure 3.73), O₁ tosses the ball high above the basket and across and off the board to the opposite side and moves over to the end of the O₄ line; O₂ times himself/herself to rebound the ball at the height of his/her jump, and flicks across high off the board to O₃, who has moved up to take the place of O₁.

The drill continues with each rebounder going quickly to the end of the opposite line as soon as he/she rebounds.

CUES: 1. Raise arms; point fingers up

2. Catch with both hands at peak of jump

Figure 3.73 (on left)
Timing across the board drill.

Figure 3.74 (on right)
Double triangle with pass drill.

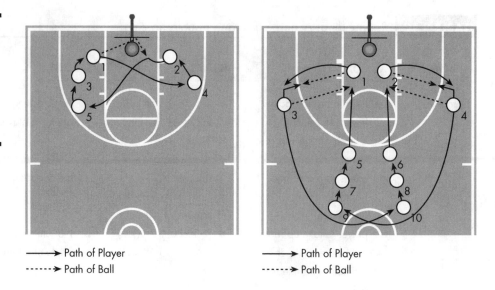

→ Path of Player
-----→ Path of Ball

→ Path of Player
-----→ Path of Ball

Drill #49: Double Triangle with Pass Drill

In the Double Triangle with Pass Drill (Figure 3.74), O_1 and O_2 each toss a ball high on the board and rebound it and pass out to the players on the side, O_3 and O_4, and take their place, then O_3 and O_4 pass to the front players in the line nearest to them, O_5 and O_6, who have moved toward the basket, and each moves out to the end of the front line farthest from them. Players O_5 and O_6 rebound their own tosses off the board and continue in the same pattern.

CUES: 1. Catch with both hands at peak of jump
2. Protect ball
3. Outlet quickly

Drill #50: Form Rebounding Drill

In the Form Rebounding Drill (Figure 3.75), two players are on each side of the lane: O_1, the rebounder, is facing O_2 on the top of the lane with the ball. To begin, O_2 throws the ball up on the backboard, then O_1 pivots, checks O_2, and jumps quickly for the rebound. The players go five times, then switch lanes and positions.

CUES: 1. Raise arms
2. Pivot and step into offensive player
3. Extend arms and jump quickly to ball
4. Catch with both hands, elbows out

Drill #51: Three-person Rebounding Drill

To perform the Three-person Rebounding Drill, S shoots the ball from at least 15 feet from the basket. D must screen out O and rebound the shot (see Figure 3.76) while O works on the offensive rebounding position. If O gets the rebound, he/she plays one-on-one against D. Once D gets the rebound, he/she becomes the next shooter by dribbling out to the wing for a shot. O now becomes the next "D" player, screening out (blocking off) S, who has become the next offensive rebounder (Figure 3.77). The drill continues until the "stop" signal is given.

CUES: 1. Raise arms
2. Block off
3. Anticipate angle of rebound

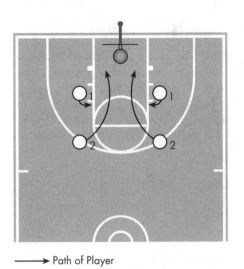

→ Path of Player

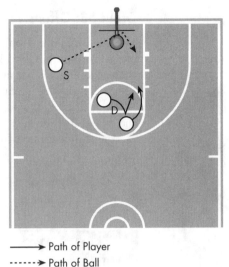

→ Path of Player

------→ Path of Ball

Figure 3.75 (on left)
Form rebounding drill.

Figure 3.76 (on right)
Three-person rebounding drill.

Drill #52: Team Blocking Off Drill

In the Team Blocking Off Drill, one team lines up in the regular offensive positions, with the defense in position. A designated shooter takes a shot from one of the outside positions as indicated by the circles in Figure 3.78. The offense works for an offensive tip or to regain possession while the defense works to get possession and complete a pass away from the defensive board for what might be the start of a break.

This drill extends the rebounding practice to a gamelike five-on-five situation. It also could be practiced by allowing the offensive players to pass the ball among the players with someone taking a jump shot within three or four passes.

CUES: 1. Block off
2. Catch at peak of jump
3. Outlet quickly

The main difference between offensive rebounding and defensive rebounding is that the offense has to move constantly to make blocking off by the defense more difficult, and the offense doesn't always have to grab the rebound but can merely tip the ball to score a basket or to keep the ball alive. The following offensive tipping drill works on this difference in rebounding offensively.

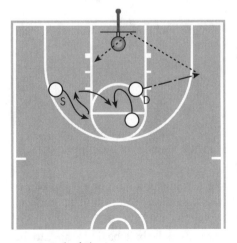

→ Path of Player

------→ Passed Ball

— · —→ Dribbled Ball

Figure 3.77 (on left)
Three-person rebounding drill with "S" as offensive rebounder.

Figure 3.78 (on right)
Team blocking off drill.

Figure 3.79
Offensive tipping drill.

⟶ Path of Player

loose ball *a situation in which neither team has possession of the ball*

traveling *taking more than one step with the ball without dribbling*

Drill #53: Offensive Tipping Drill

For the Offensive Tipping Drill, players 1 and 2 take positions as shown in Figure 3.79. Player 3 takes a quick set or jump shot and then rebounds his/her area, as do 1 and 2. The three of them keep after the ball until making the basket. The ball then is passed out to 4, who has taken the place of 3, with 5 moving up and 1 moving to the end of the line as 2 takes the place of 1 and 3 takes the place of 2. The drill continues, following this pattern.

CUES: 1. Move
2. Raise arms
3. Tip ball toward basket

SKILL 12 | Control of Loose Balls

A **loose ball** usually is caused by smart, aggressive, defensive play. If the defense deflects a pass or blocks a shot, the end result is often a situation where the ball is free and either team may gain possession of it. Loose balls are the result of poor offensive play when an offensive player makes an errant pass that goes to no one in particular, or the ball might be dribbled off an offensive player's foot, or a pass might be fumbled. In any of these situations, each team has to try to gain possession of the ball and prepare to make the transition from offense to defense, or vice versa.

To get loose or free balls, players must be aggressive. Keys to obtaining possession of a loose ball are speed and the willingness to do almost anything to get the ball. Diving on the floor to recover the ball is an example. The following suggestions can help in recovering loose balls.

1. Keep in mind that your teammates will help on defense (transition) if you fail to get the ball.
2. When diving for a loose ball, don't foul unnecessarily. Go for the ball, not a player.
3. If you cannot get the loose ball, block or screen an opponent to allow one of your teammates more opportunity to get the ball.
4. When you get possession of the ball, immediately yell "ball" so the offense can start at once (transition).
5. When you secure a loose ball, don't get excited and take a poor shot or make a bad pass.

CUES: 1. Stay in a crouched position—knees bent, hips low
2. Scoop the ball with the closest hand
3. Pull the ball to the other hand
4. Pivot away from opposition
5. Keep chin up

When the situation dictates diving for a ball:

1. Dive and roll. This will allow you to fall in such a way as not to injure yourself.
2. Keep your chin up.
3. Hold the ball. If you can't get the ball to a teammate, a hold or a jump ball is better than allowing the other team to gain possession. You cannot get back up to your feet. That would be a **traveling** violation.
4. Begin the transition. If you are not the player getting the ball, begin to move to the defense or offense, as appropriate, to be a step ahead of the imminent transition.

Loose Ball Drills

Typically, two players are going after a loose ball. The player who gets the ball drives for the basket while his/her counterpart becomes a defensive player. The following drills are aimed at retrieving loose balls and beginning the transition from defense to offense.

Drill #54: Dive Drill

The coach/teacher starts the Dive Drill by rolling the ball to about the head of the key at an angle shown in Figure 3.80. Player O_1 sprints, dives, and deflects the ball up ahead to teammate O_2; O_2 scoops up the ball on the run and dribbles to the basket for a lay-up. Player O_1 gets up quickly and sprints after the shooter to tap into a possible missed shot. The players go to the ends of opposite lines at the other end of the court. This drill can be run on both sides of the floor at the same time.

CUES: 1. Crouched position
       2. Keep chin up
       3. Tap ball up court
       4. Get up quickly, and follow

Drill #55: Loose Ball Break Drill

In the Loose Ball Break Drill, three pairs of players have their backs facing the coach/teacher on the baseline. The coach/teacher calls "ball" and rolls the ball. All players turn and fight for possession of the ball. The team that recovers the ball is on offense and the other on defense. Offensive players should fill the three lanes (see Figure 3.81) and fast break (discussed next) to the other end. Defensive players should get back as quickly as possible.

CUES: 1. Keep chin up
       2. Protect ball or pass
       3. Fill lane

SKILL 13   Fast Breaks

The transition skills included in this section are:

- Fast break—changing from defense to offense
- Defending the break—changing from offense to defense

The objective of the **fast break** is to go down court and take a high-percentage shot before the defense has an opportunity to set up. This requires one team to change quickly from a defensive posture to offense and try to beat the other team down the court. This transition from defense to offense usually is the result of a defensive rebound, an intercepted pass or a stolen ball, gaining possession of a loose ball, or from a blocked shot.

Defending the break requires one team who had previous possession of the ball to change quickly from offense to defense to

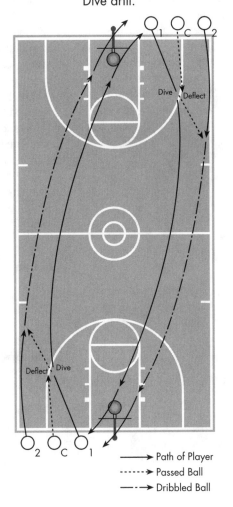

Figure 3.80
Dive drill.

Dive   Deflect
Deflect   Dive

⟶ Path of Player
┈┈▸ Passed Ball
─·─▸ Dribbled Ball

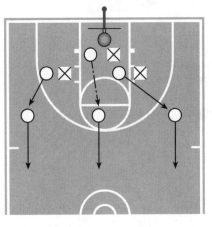

Figure 3.81
Loose ball break drill.

⟶ Path of Player
─·─▸ Dribbled Ball

fast break a situation in which the defensive team gains possession of the ball and moves quickly into scoring position so team members outnumber opponents; the idea is to attempt to score before the opponent's defense can be set up

disrupt or challenge the fast-breaking team. This transition consists of getting back and protecting one's own goal. Table 3.14 provides a summary of fast break and defending-the-break skills.

Basketball is a fast-paced game with plenty of action. The fast break ensures that the pace of the game will remain quick and full of excitement. Today's players and spectators like to play and watch teams execute the fast break. Perhaps nothing is more exciting in the game of basketball than to have a team make a basket quickly and efficiently as the result of the fast break.

The fast break is a well-organized attack that can originate from any part of the court and from many different circumstances. A break (transition) may occur after a missed shot (defensive rebound), upon gaining possession of a loose ball, from an intercepted pass, or from a blocked shot. Each player is responsible for recognizing the transition that is about to take place and capitalizing on the situation.

The fast break is a definite pattern looking for an unbalanced defense. Most fast-break opportunities are made in the back court. The following guidelines should be considered in executing the fast break:

1. Start the break with a quick pass to a player on the same side on which the ball is recovered.
2. End the break with a high-percentage shot.
3. Get the ball down the floor as quickly as possible using either the pass (the quickest way) or by dribbling.

TABLE 3.14 Fast break and defending-the-break summary

TRANSITION	FUNDAMENTALS	OBJECTIVE
Fast break	Quick ball handling	Short passes with little dribbling to get the ball up court quickly
	Quick, high percentage, shooting	Lay-ups, baby hooks, and short jumpers should be recognized
	Primary break	Ball should be in middle of court with players on each wing for balance
	Secondary break	If initial break is halted, a secondary break can follow
	Two-on-one situations	Spreading out so both breakers cannot be guarded
	Three-on-two situations	Ball in middle and wings spread so all three players cannot be guarded
		Trailer is responsible to follow in all situations
Defending the Break	Getting back	To disrupt the flow of the offensive fast break
	Defense: Two-on-one situations	Don't concede any baskets
	Defense: Three-on-two situations	Stall the offense until help arrives
	Defense: Four-on-three situations	

trailer fourth player in the fast break who "trails" the primary break and becomes important if the three fillers don't score. Used as a secondary option in the fast break

4. Don't run away from the ball unless the defense attempts to pinch off passes.

5. Keep your balance. Keep the ball in the middle of the floor with a cutter on each side and a trailer following the play.

6. If you are the player with the ball, make the defense defend the ball.

7. Use deception in ball handling.

8. Hold up as a team in a 15-foot triangle position unless there is an opening to go all the way to the basket.

Mistakes will occur in this fast-paced style of play. Practice will help in executing the break, and players may learn that organization is more important than sheer speed.

Quick shooting and fast *ball handling* fundamentals have to be practiced and drilled again and again. Generally, the cues for the jump shot and the lay-up apply to quick shooting. The only real difference is the pace or speed at which they are practiced. The idea is to get maximum speed with control. The same is true for all ball handling fundamentals. Hard driving shots under pressure and quick jump shots must be executed properly.

Although the fast break starts when a team is playing defense, the transition to the fast break offense can begin from many situations. An intercepted pass, stolen ball, blocked shot, and even a made basket can be the beginning of the transition from defense to an offensive fast break. The most common scenario, however, is the break started from a missed shot. This requires a defensive rebound. A player can't run the break without the ball. Next, a quick outlet pass to a ball handler will start the quick transition from defense to offense and, hopefully, provide the advantage of having more offensive players than defensive players. The ball should get to the middle of the court as soon as possible. The ball should be passed forward with as little dribbling as possible. The lanes should be filled, and a trailer and protector should follow the play.

In the *primary break* five players have to be sure that all five positions or responsibilities of the fast break are "filled." Specifically, the ball should be in the middle of the floor between the two sidelines. There should be a cutter or wing on each side of the ball. Having one wing slightly ahead of the ball and one slightly behind the ball is most desirable. These three "lanes"—ball handler in the middle and two wings—make up the primary part of the break.

The middle player or ball handler is the key to success of the break. This player must be clever, to get the ball to the right place at the right time. The middle player must keep his/her head and eyes up, preparing to get the ball down the floor to a teammate in the most advantageous position as quickly as possible. A quick pass is the best method of advancing the ball; however, if this cannot be done safely, the middle player should drive hard on the dribble. Passing to a teammate who is moving toward a sideline or to a corner is not recommended.

If the ball handler is driving toward the basket on the dribble, he/she should penetrate to the free throw area about 15 feet from the basket. If the player has an easy chance to score, he/she can go deeper.

The cutters or wings should cut from the sidelines or corner to receive a pass from the middle player. The cuts should be at a sharp angle, not in arcs. The wings must set up a defensive player to get open; therefore, change of pace and direction facilitate receiving the pass from the middle man and scoring an easy basket. The cutters also should hold up or not penetrate farther than the inside rebound positions on the free throw lane. Therefore, these three players form a 15-foot triangle. This will keep the basket area from being crowded and will prevent the defense from covering more than one player at a time.

Ideally, the middle player will pass to a cutter on either side. Upon making the pass, the middle player should take one step toward the receiver with hands up, ready to take a quick return pass. If the pass is not returned, the middle player looks to rebound if a shot is taken. The other cutter gets position to rebound on his/her side of the basket.

The middle player, upon passing, also may screen for the trailer, take a jump shot from the foul circle area, or drive down the lane if the defense is out of position. The cutters always should consider rebound positioning if they don't receive the ball.

Two-on-One Situations

two-on-one situation
one in which two offensive players have an advantage over the one defender during a fast break

In a **two-on-one situation,** illustrated in Figure 3.82, the offensive players should spread out (about 12–15 feet) while passing the ball back and forth as they move down the floor. This will prevent the single defender from guarding both offensive players.

The offensive players should watch the defender and make him/her commit to defend one player or the other. The first offensive player who has the opportunity should drive to the basket. If he/she cannot complete a lay-up, he/she should pass to the teammate. The goal is for one offensive player to make an uncontested lay-up while the teammate follows for a tip or an offensive rebound.

Three-on-Two Situations

three-on-two situation
one in which three offensive players have an advantage over two defenders during a fast break

In a **three-on-two situation,** illustrated in Figure 3.83, the offensive players should get the ball into the middle of the court, preferably to a ball handler. The two cutters or wings should cut sharply to the basket at the free throw line extended. The middle player should penetrate to foul line area but no deeper unless an uncontested lay-up is available. The cutter pulls up at the foul lane rebounding position if

Figure 3.82

Two-on-one situation.

The two offensive players should spread out while passing from side to side and moving down the floor. In this way, the single defensive man will not know which one to guard.

Figure 3.83
Three-on-two situation.

he/she does not receive a pass from the ball handler. This creates a triangle with the offensive players spread about 15 feet apart. If one defensive player comes out to the foul line, an offensive player will be free for a lay-up.

Secondary Breaks

The trailer's responsibilities is to watch the fast break develop and cut into open areas around the basket. This is known as the **secondary break.** If the cutters do not get a lay-up or short jump shot, the trailer gives the offense another option to get an easy basket by coming down the lane after the primary options are stopped. By going down the lane, the trailer also can become an offensive rebounder or get a tip shot if one of the cutters or middle players takes a shot. Many times the trailer can go all the way to the basket without being checked by the defense.

The fifth player is known as the *protector*. His/her responsibilities include being the first back on defense if something goes wrong during the break and the other team begins a break of its own. Also, the protector watches the break develop and moves behind the ball to a distance of about 15 feet. This puts the protector in position to receive the ball and begin to execute the "set offense" if the break is negated by the defense.

Because of the nature of the fast break, many errors, both mechanical and mental, are likely to occur. Dribbling instead of passing the ball down the court can allow the defense time to get back and stop the advantages of the fast break. Over-passing instead of shooting can give the defense time to set up or disrupt the break. Not filling the lanes or not getting the ball into the middle of the court can create an unbalanced offense that may negate any offensive advantage. The absence of a trailer may prevent an easy secondary break opportunity or prevent a possible offensive rebound and second-shot opportunity. Finally, poor fundamentals in exe-

secondary break *second options for scoring during a fast break if primary options are stopped; usually the trailer is the player designated for these "second options"*

Figure 3.84

Finish of the fast break.

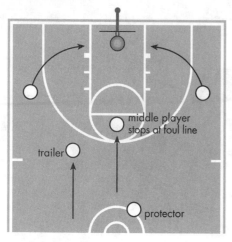

⟶ Path of Player

cuting passing, receiving, shooting, and dribbling at a fast pace may mean mishandled balls or low percentage shots, which ultimately leads to the opponents gaining possession of the ball without the breaking team scoring points.

Figure 3.84 depicts the conclusion of the fast break. Table 3.15 summarizes the execution, cues, errors, and causes of errors for the fast break.

Fast Break Drills

The fast break, or the transition from defense to offense, is the beginning of offensive play and, for some, the beginning of patterned play. To practice the break, the concept of "building the fast break" should be considered. This "building" is a sequential progression that starts with one-on-one situations and grows into a five-player break with all players responsible for specific duties (cutters, trailer, protector). Many excellent drills are available for practicing the fast break. The drills presented here are intended to stress the "building" concept and emphasize the situation breaks, such as the two-on-one and three-on-two breaks.

TABLE 3.15	Fast breaks: Action, cues, and troubleshooting.			
FAST BREAK SITUATIONS	**BIOMECHANICAL ACTIONS**	**VERBAL CUES**	**ERRORS**	**CAUSES OF ERRORS**
Primary break	■ Get defensive rebound ■ Make quick outlet pass to a ball handler ■ Get the ball into the middle of the court as soon as possible ■ Pass the ball down court with as little dribbling as possible ■ Fill the lanes. Ball in middle; cutters on each side ■ Trailer follows play for secondary break opportunities ■ Protector or fifth player provides line of defense if errors are made ■ Take high percentage shots	■ Get ball ■ Quick outlet pass ■ Ball in middle of court ■ Pass before dribble ■ Fill lanes for balance ■ Take high percentage shots	1. Turnovers 2. Unbalanced floor 3. Missed shots 4. Allow defense to catch up or establish position	1. Poor ball handling at a fast pace 2. Ball not in middle or lanes not filled 3. Poor shot selection 4. Overpassing, dribbling too deep, congestion in lane

(continued)

TABLE 3.15 Continued.

Two-on-one	■ Two offensive players spread out 12–15 feet ■ Pass ball back and forth ■ Drive to basket at first opportunity or when defense commits ■ Shoot an uncontested lay-up or pass to teammate	■ Spread out ■ Pass back and forth ■ Drive for lay-up	1. Defense able to guard both players 2. Missed shots	1. Offensive tandem not spread; ball not kept moving back and forth 2. Poor shot selection; not reacting to defense pressure
Three-on-two	■ Get ball in a ball handler's control in middle of court ■ Fill both outside lanes ■ Cutters (wings) should make sharp cuts at free throw line extended ■ Ball handler (middle player) should pull up at foul line area or go for an uncontested lay-up ■ Cutters shoot lay-up or short jumpers if they receive ball ■ If not, pull up at free throw rebound position to form a three-player triangle (15 feet apart) ■ When defense commits, move ball to open teammate	■ Get ball to middle ■ Fill lanes ■ Cut sharply to basket ■ Penetrate to foul-line area and pass	1. Defense able to guard all three players 2. Missed shots	1. Offense didn't form 15-foot triangle 2. Poor shot selection, not reacting to defensive pressure
Secondary break	■ Trailer follows play ■ Keep head, eyes, hands up ■ Cut to open areas around basket ■ Shoot lay-up, short jumper, or tip rebound	■ Follow break down middle of court ■ Keep head, eyes, hands up ■ Cut through lane to basket	1. No offensive rebound or tip 2. No secondary options	1. No trailer 2. Trailer not ready for pass, shot, etc.

Figure 3.85

One-on-one drill with trailer.

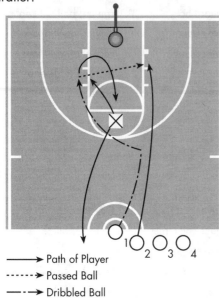

——→ Path of Player
------→ Passed Ball
—·—→ Dribbled Ball

Drill #56: One-on-One Drill with Trailer

In the One-on-One Drill with Trailer (Figure 3.85), Player 1 tries to score on X. Player 1 should make fast moves as if X has help coming. X tries to delay Player 1 and force a bad shot or a turnover. Player 2 waits until 1 dribbles to the top of the circle, then trails the play. Player 1 can either shoot or pass to 2 if X stops the penetration. If 2 does not receive a pass, he/she should go to the basket for a tip try or to collect an offensive rebound and a second-chance score. At the end of the drill, Player 1 becomes the defender (X), and X and 2 return to the end of the offensive line, where 2 will be the ball handler and X will be a trailer.

CUES (Trailer):

1. Keep head, eyes, hands up
2. Look for pass and high-percentage shots
3. Go for tip, or try for rebound

CUES (Ball handler):

1. Move quickly; don't hesitate
2. Take high-percentage shots
3. Pass if no shot is available
4. Look for return pass

Drill #57: Two-on-One Drill

In the Two-on-One Drill (Figure 3.86), Players 1 and 2 attack the defensive player (X). Players 1 and 2 should be 12 to 15 feet apart and should pass the ball back and forth until one of them has the opportunity to drive to the basket. If the defensive player picks up and defends the driver, a pass should be made to the teammate. In this drill, the goal is to make a lay-up shot.

CUES:
1. Spread out
2. Pass quickly back and forth
3. Drive for lay-up, offensive rebounding

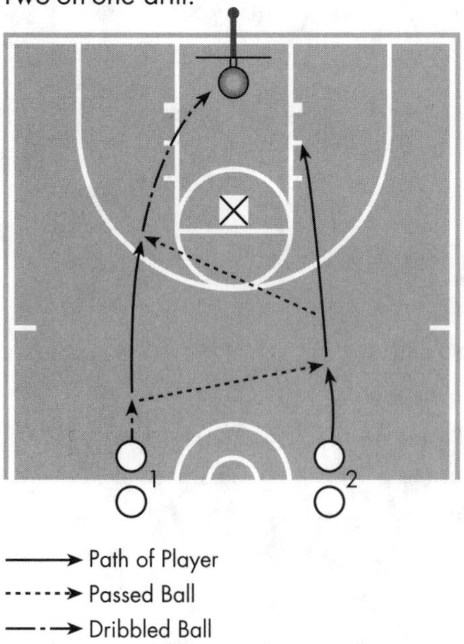

Drill #58: Three-on-Two, Two-on-One Break Drill

To begin the Three-on-Two, Two-on-One Break Drill, Player O_1 has the ball in the middle with Players O_2 and O_3 in the outside lanes. Players X_1 and X_2 are defenders positioned in the lane (Figure 3.87a). The O's attack the X's and try to score three versus two. When X secures a rebound from either a missed shot or a made shot, the X's go two on one toward the other basket. Player O_1 becomes the defender and must get back (Figure 3.87b). Players O_2 and O_3 will become the new defenders (X's) at the original end of the court. A new group of three brings the ball up after the two-on-one break is completed. This is a continuous drill.

CUES
1. Get ball to middle
2. Fill lanes
3. Make sharp cuts to basket
4. Penetrate foul-line area and pass

Figure 3.86

Two-on-one drill.

——→ Path of Player
------→ Passed Ball
—·—→ Dribbled Ball

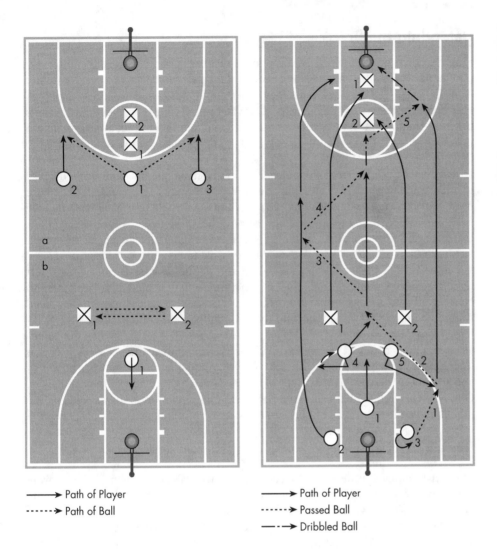

Figure 3.87 (on left)
Three-on-two, two-on-one break.

Figure 3.88 (on right)
Five-on-two drill.

———➤ Path of Player
------➤ Path of Ball

———➤ Path of Player
------➤ Passed Ball
—·—➤ Dribbled Ball

Drill #59: Five-on-Two Drill

In the Five-on-Two Drill (Figure 3.88), Player X_1 or X_2 shoots an outside shot, O_4 and O_5 block X's away from basket, and then get in position to receive an outlet pass. Players 1, 2, and 3 form a rebound triangle in front of the basket to get the defensive rebound. If 3 rebounds, he/she makes an outlet pass to 5 (same side as rebound), and 5 passes to 4, who fills the middle lane. Then 5 fills the right outside lane, 2 fills the left outside lane, and 1 comes out the middle trailing 4 by at least 15 feet (trailer). Player 3 becomes the protector and trails 1 by 15 feet.

The X's get back on defense to disrupt the break. More defensive players can be added to this drill, but five-on-four usually is the highest number of defenders used in this drill.

CUES: 1. Get rebound (ball)

2. Outlet pass

3. Get ball to middle

4. Fill lanes

5. Take high-percentage shot

6. Look for trailer

Defending the Break

Slowing down or eliminating an opponent's fast break can change the complexity of a game. Teams that get back and protect their defensive basket typically do not give up "easy baskets" and, thus, they make the opposition earn all of its points. Fast-breaking teams, on the other hand, are attempting to get as many easy baskets as possible and control the tempo or pace of the game. Therefore, all teams should practice the transition skills of getting back on defense so they will be prepared to defend against the fast break.

Just as the offense needs to understand how to make the transition from defense to offense and what to do if a two-on-one or three-on-two situation arises, the defense must consider the same transitions. The basic fundamentals of getting back include assigning responsibility to specific players or defining procedures for players to follow under different situations so someone is always back to defend against the break. Getting back is about hustle and knowledge of what to do under certain situations.

Specifically, defensive players should run to the defensive end of the court until they have caught up to the ball. At that point, they should do a half-turn and back-pedal into defensive position (the back to the defensive basket). The head should be up, the player should find the ball, and should communicate his/her intentions to their teammates. If a player already is ahead of the ball when the defensive rebound is made, he/she should back-pedal from half-court. If a two-on-one or three-on-two situation arises, the defensive players should take up their positions and attempt to disrupt the break (see later discussion on Individual Defense Skills). Other defensive fast break specifics include stopping the outlet pass, pressing the rebounder, and stopping the in-bounds pass.

Drill #60: Get-Back Drill

The Get-Back Drill is designed to teach players to recover as a team and take away opponents' fast break. Three defensive players (X) take a position in a triangle under the basket. Two defensive players are at half-court on the sideline on each side. The five offensive players (O) make from three to five passes, then take a shot. The defense makes an outlet pass to half-court. The half-court player hits the opposite player on the sideline for an attempted lay-up. Five defensive players now must get back and stop the lay-up. No one can release until the rebound. Figure 3.89 illustrates this sequence.

Figure 3.89
Get-back drill.

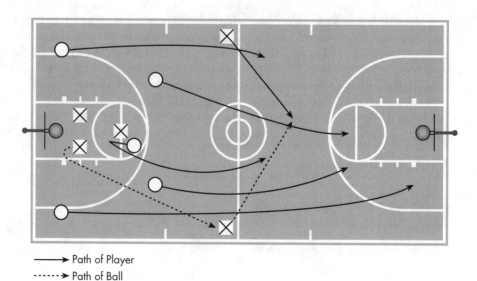

⎯⎯→ Path of Player
------→ Path of Ball

CUES: 1. Run to assigned area
2. Find the ball
3. Back-pedal into position

Drill #61: Seven-on-Five Get-Back Drill

In the Seven-on-Five Get-Back Drill (Figure 3.90), the X's (defensive fast-break team) run their various offensive options. If they score they get the ball again at mid-court. If a field goal attempt is missed or the defense (the O numbers) recovers the ball by a rebound or an interception, the X's retreat immediately to defense, and the initial defensive team (the O numbers) fast breaks to the opposite end of the floor. The fast break team has an added advantage because, as soon as the ball changes hands, players 6 and 7 (who are on opposite sidelines from each other at mid-court) sprint to the other end of the floor and join the other five numbered players in a seven-on-five fast break. This drill can be a pressure-simulated, competitive game by keeping score:

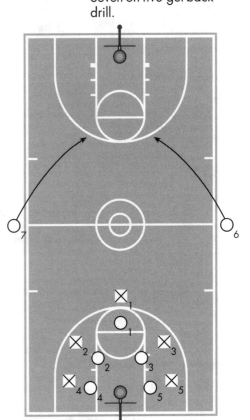

Figure 3.90
Seven-on-five get-back drill.

X's score = basket (1 point), free throw (1 point), offensive rebound (1 point), stop fast break attempt (1 point)

O's score = drawing a foul (5 points), scoring on fast break (5 points), and offensive rebound (1 point)

CUES: 1. Find ball
2. Run to defensive end
3. Back-pedal into position

| **SKILL** | **14** | **Defense Fundamentals** |

The individual defensive fundamentals included in this section are:

- Defensive stance/position
- Defending the ball handler
- Defending a player without the ball
- Defending when outnumbered

Defensive play requires hard work, determination, and lots of hustle. Fundamentals of the defensive stance require the players to get their buttocks down and head up, and be ready to keep their feet moving.

The first and primary responsibility of defense is to stop the ball. Therefore, defending the dribbler, potential shooter, and passer from many different court positions and potential situations are included in the discussion of defending the ball handler.

Just as important as defending the ball, and necessary for good team defense, is the ability to defend players away from the ball. Those players usually are one pass away from being potential shooters or ball handlers. They always are potential cutters or screeners.

Finally, some defensive situations in basketball require the defense to play when it is outnumbered (more offense than defensive players). Defense funda-

INDIVIDUAL DEFENSE SKILLS

TABLE 3.16 Individual defensive fundamentals.

CONDITION/SITUATION	OBJECTIVE
Defensive stance/position	To be ready to move to deny the offense any advantage
	To stay between your opponent and the basket
	To keep good balance, relaxed, and ready
Defending the ball handler	To be aggressive and dominate your opponent
	To force a dribbler away from the basket toward the sideline, corner, or congested area
	To impair the accuracy of a shooter and to deny position
Defending a player without the ball	To prevent your opponent from receiving or having possession of the ball in an area close to basket where he/she is a threat as a shooter, dribble driver, or passer-cutter
	To disrupt the flow of the offensive fast break
Defending when outnumbered	To stall offense until help arrives

Figure 3.91

Defensive stance.

In the defensive stance:

- Bend knees for balance and quick movement
- Place feet apart, slightly more than shoulder width
- Keep head and chin up
- Raise arm to distract shooter
- Spread arms to deflect possible pass

mentals are mandatory when a player is alone defending against two or three offensive players or when two defenders are against three offensive players.

Defense can be the glue that holds a team together. Defensive fundamentals are just as valuable as offensive skills. Table 3.16 provides a summary of individual defensive fundamentals.

The following guidelines pertain to playing aggressive, hard-nosed defense, regardless of the specific basketball situation.

1. Keep between your opponent and his/her basket.
2. Play defense with your head and feet.
3. Play your best defense before your opponent receives the ball.
4. Keep the ball and your opponent within your sight at all times possible.
5. Keep your weight back and your center of gravity low.
6. Don't cross your legs; slide instead.
7. Play the opponent, not the ball.
8. Don't leave your feet unless the ball or your opponent is in the air.
9. Don't quit. Keep trying. Always hustle.
10. Study your opponent to discover specific strengths and weaknesses.
11. Know the system of play the opposing team uses.
12. Help your teammates. Talk it up.

Defensive Stance/Position

Many basketball players have trouble understanding the importance of staying low and maintaining a certain stance when playing defense. If a player is already quicker and more skilled than his/her opponent, a player often can get away with playing defense without using good fundamentals. Players quickly learn, however, that as skill level and quickness become more even among opponents, the player who has a good defense stance and position will have the advantage.

The defensive stance (Figure 3.91) requires the player to keep his/her weight back and the center of gravity low. The knees should be bent, the back straight, and the hips and buttocks low. The head and chin should be up so the eyes can look through the opponent at chest level. The feet are spread apart, slightly more than the width of the shoulders, and the heels barely touch the floor.

One foot and one hand should be forward (*ipsalateral,* or same-sided). The inside foot and the other hand point toward the ball if the opponent does not have the ball. The forward hand should wave to distract the offensive player but the player should not reach with it. The other hand feels behind the player toward the basket when the opponent has the ball. The player should feel comfortable.

The player also should consider the position on the court he/she occupies while assuming the proper defensive stance. (Generally, the leg on the strong or danger side of the person the player is defending is split.) As a general rule, the inside leg is kept forward and the outside leg back when the opponent has the ball. Also, the player should judge distance he/she should be away from the opponent according to how far he/she is from the ball and from the basket. Finally, the player should try to maintain a position that will make it as difficult as possible for the opponent to receive a pass in an area where he/she can shoot, drive, or pass.

When moving, the basic position (stance) does not change. The body remains low, and the feet never cross. Sliding the feet and maintaining good balance are essential. Among the most common mistakes when defending an opponent one-on-one result from not maintaining a good defensive stance and positioning. This allows the offensive player to gain an advantage because when the player is off-balance, the ball handler can get past him/her more easily. Also, the opponent knows what he/she wants to do before the defender does, giving him/her a mental advantage. Reaching with the hands can cause the defender to lose his/her balance and give up good position.

Two types of steps or slides allow the defender to move efficiently and quickly while not changing the basic position or stance. The **slide step,** sometimes called the side step (shown in Figure 3.92) is executed by moving the feet into a parallel

slide step *a defensive step that allows quick changes of direction by moving the feet into a parallel stance with both feet in line with the direction the player is going*

a   b

Figure 3.92
Slide step (slide).

Figure 3.93
Drop step.

drop step *a defensive step that allows the defender to regain or maintain good positioning by doing reverse pivot with back foot and stepping back with lead foot*

stance with both feet in line with the direction the player is going (a). The defender should push off the foot farthest from the direction he/she is going and step with the near foot (b). The feet should never cross and the defender should maintain balance to allow for quick changes of direction.

The **drop step** and slide (Figure 3.93) is useful when an offensive player attempts to drive by the defender on the side of the defender's lead foot. Moving backward in the direction of the lead foot is difficult when a defender is in the basic stance. The drop step allows the defender to regain or maintain good defensive positioning.

The drop step is executed by doing a reverse pivot with the back foot and stepping back (dropping) with the lead foot. The drop step should be straight back in the direction of the opponent's movement. The defender should keep his/her eyes on the opponent at all times and push off of the back foot toward the drop step. This allows the defender to use the slide step to regain defensive positioning. The defender should never turn his/her back on the opponent in an attempt to regain defensive positioning.

Table 3.17 summarizes the defensive stance and possible errors in executing the fundamentals of individual defense.

TABLE 3.17 Defensive stance and basic positioning: Action, cues, and troubleshooting.

BIOMECHANICAL ACTION	VERBAL CUES	ERRORS	CAUSES OF ERRORS
Keep between opponent and his/her basket	Keep head and chin up	Lose balance	Poor stance
Keep the ball and opponent within sight at all times	Bend knees; keep hips and buttocks low		Reaching with hands; not moving feet
Keep your weight back and center of gravity low	Keep back straight		Crossing legs
Bend knees, keep the back straight, and keep the hips and buttocks low	Spread feet; inside leg forward, outside leg back		
Keep head and chin up— look through the opponent	Spread arms		
Place feet slightly more than shoulders-width apart with heels barely touching the floor	Slide feet		
Keep inside leg forward, outside leg back; split the leg on opponent's strong side			
Extend one hand forward (same hand as forward leg); point other hand to ball			
Slide feet without crossing legs			

Defending the Ball Handler

When defending a dribbler (see Figure 3.94), the primary task is to drive him/her away from the basket, preferably toward a sideline, corner, or congested area. This will give the defense an advantage in terms of court space or double-teaming opportunities. As the defender moves with the dribbler, he/she should stay low and slide the feet so he/she is just ahead of the dribbler. The only time crossing the legs is acceptable is if the dribbler gets by the player and he/she has to sprint to catch up.

The defender should focus on the dribbler's chest (midsection). The ball handler can't fake with this part of his/her body and can't go anywhere without the midsection.

Defense is played with the feet and good positioning, not by stopping and reaching with the hands. The near hand is used to play the ball from underneath and flip the fingers and wrist toward the defender. The defender should never slap down at the ball. This will almost always result in a foul being called against the defense.

Figure 3.94

Defending the dribbler.

Keep a step ahead of dribbler to guard against drive   Slide feet

If the dribbler picks up the ball, the defender should advance quickly and get "on top" of the opponent to deny shooting opportunities and to make passing off more difficult. The defensive player should try to force the ball handler to pass away from the basket.

The defensive player should study the tendencies of the opponent. If he/she dribbles with only one hand or obviously prefers one hand, always goes to the same side, does not like pressure, or usually passes or shoots off the dribble, the defensive player can take advantage of this knowledge and turn his/her tendencies into defensive assets.

If the ball handler becomes a passer or potential shooter, the following fundamentals apply.

When defending a passer, the player keeps his/her hand down on the side where there is danger that he/she might drive. The other hand stays up and moves in the direction that a pass is likely to go. If the dribble is lost or used up, the defensive player gets in tight and attempts to destroy the passer's vision.

When defending a potential shooter, the player puts a hand up in his/her face to distract the shot if he/she is in shooting range. If the player is not in range, the hands should be low. A hand should always be up and waving when the shooters range is in doubt.

Defensive players should not leave their feet unless the ball and the shooter are in the air already. The defender should be the last player off the ground. In addition, the defender should go straight up and not slap down in an attempt to block a shot. The near hand should be used when attempting to block the driving shot. The defender also should block off or check the shooter after the shot to keep the shooter from getting the offensive rebound.

If the ball handler is attempting to use a screen to free himself/herself from the defender, the defender should open up toward the screen. This means having the shoulders square (perpendicular) to and the head facing the screen. The defensive player also takes a step toward the far side of the ball handler. This maneuver helps the defender avoid the screen and allows good vision to anticipate the ball handler's next move. This procedure should be used on side screens and blind or rear screens. The defender should try to force the ball handler to a congested area where he/she can get help from teammates.

The defender must be alert constantly and have total concentration. Otherwise errors in defense will occur when defending the ball handler. Watching the ball or taking a head, eyes, or other fakes can cause the defender to lose position. Slapping and reaching in with the hands often causes the defender to stop moving his/her feet, which almost always gives the ball handler an advantage. Leaving the feet before the shooter or before the ball is in the air gives the offense the advantage. Finally, slapping down on the ball for a steal attempt or a blocked shot attempt is almost always called a foul and will give the offense free throw opportunities. Table 3.18 summarizes defending the ball handler, potential passer, and shooter, and gives a troubleshooting guide for defensive errors.

TABLE 3.18 Defending the ball handler: Action, cues, and troubleshooting.

DEFENSIVE CONDITION	BIOMECHANICAL ACTION	VERBAL CUES	ERRORS	CAUSES OF ERRORS
Defending the dribbler	■ Stay low and slide the feet	■ Get a step ahead	1. Lose positioning	1. Not keeping feet moving; staying low; taking fakes; reaching with hands
	■ Stay a step ahead of the dribbler	■ Slide feet; stay low	2. Fouling	2. Slapping down on ball; reaching with far hand
	■ Stay a step ahead of the dribbler	■ Slide feet; stay low	3. Allowing an easy pass or basket	3. Not getting on top or closing in on dribbler when dribble is picked up
	■ Focus eyes on dribbler's midsection	■ Focus on midsection		
	■ Use near hand to play ball from underneath; flip wrist and fingers toward body	■ Don't reach ■ Get on top		
	■ If dribble is fast, get up tight to dribbler			
Defending the passer	■ Keep hands down on sides where the ball handler has potential to drive	■ Hands: one up, one down	1. Allowing an easy pass	1. Not tightening up space between you and the ball handler
	■ Keep other hand up, moving in direction of potential pass	■ Destroy vision	2. Fouling	2. Slapping down at ball; not waving hand to distract
	■ If dribble is lost, move in tight and disrupt passer's vision			

(continued)

TABLE 3.18	Continued.			
DEFENSIVE CONDITION	**BIOMECHANICAL ACTION**	**VERBAL CUES**	**ERRORS**	**CAUSES OF ERRORS**
Defending the shooter	■ Put a hand in shooter's face	■ Hand in face	1. Allowing an uncontested shot	1. Not tightening up space
	■ Keep hands moving even if not shooting	■ Second to leave floor	2. Taking fake	2. Leaving floor before shot/shooter
	■ Stay on floor until shot is in the air	■ Go straight up	3. Fouling	3. Jumping into shooter; slapping down on ball while it is in shooter's hand
	■ Go straight up	■ Use near hand		
	■ Don't slap down to block a shot			
	■ Use near hand to block shots			
Avoiding the screener	■ Open up toward screener; shoulders perpendicular to screener	■ Open up	1. Caught in screen	1. Not opening up to see screen
	■ Step toward ball handler's far side	■ Step to opposite side		
	■ Force ball handler to congested area; don't allow ball handler to go where he/she wants	■ Drive to help		

Defending a Player Without the Ball

A fundamental to playing effective individual defense is not to permit an offensive player to receive the ball in an advantageous position (Figure 3.95). Unfortunately, many players begin to play defense only when the opponent has the ball. The offensive player usually does *not* have the ball, so most of the defensive work is done against a player without the ball.

The main objective of good individual defense is to prevent the opponent from receiving or having possession of the ball in an area close enough to the basket where he/she is a threat to score, dribble, or pass. The defender has to stay between the opponent and the basket. This simple fundamental can help the defender have good position and deny the offensive player access to position on the court.

Equally important is to keep one hand pointing toward the ball and the other hand pointing toward the opponent whenever a teammate has the ball. This will help the defender to see both the ball and the player being defended. Losing sight of one or the other can be detrimental to successful defense, so **peripheral vision** is important. Other considerations are keeping the basic defensive stance and play-

peripheral vision ability to see to the side while looking ahead

Prevent the pass by keeping the body between passer and receiver

Defensive player prevents reverse cut to basket by keeping his left arm near the offensive player

Figure 3.95
Denying the offensive player the ball.

ing the passing lane between the ball and the offensive player. When defending a cutter, the player should try to make him/her catch the ball going away from the basket or toward a sideline. The defender should anticipate the give-and-go move by the offense and keep moving. Finally, the defender should block out the opponent when a shot is taken, and go after the ball. Table 3.19 summarizes specific fundamentals for defending the wing, guard, and post players when they do not have the ball. Figure 3.96 shows how to guard a post player.

Defending When Outnumbered

In basketball, "having numbers" refers to the situation in which the offense has more players attacking the basket than the defense has in defending it. The most common situations are two-on-one, three-on-two, and four-on-three. Even though the offense has a decided advantage by having at least one more player available than the defense does to execute its offense, the defense can follow basic fundamentals that will give it an honest chance at thwarting the offensive thrust. Generally, the defense hopes to disrupt the offensive execution so it commits a turnover, or hopes to stall the offense until defensive help arrives.

In two-on-one situations, the lone defender should position himself/herself near the free throw line area and open up so he/she can see both oncoming offensive players. Ideally, if the ball can be stopped around the foul line, this may allow time for help to arrive to defend the other player. The player without the ball, however, is the more dangerous of the two, so the defender cannot leave him or her uncovered.

The defender should keep the arm and leg back on the side where the offensive player without the ball is. If the player with the ball pulls up or loses the dribble, the defender should back up quickly to defend the extra offensive player. After a shot is taken, the defensive player must rebound. A good offensive stance and balance, plus mentally anticipating the offensive play, can give the lane defender an excellent chance to disrupt the play.

TABLE 3.19	Defending post players, wings, and guards without the ball: Action, cues, and troubleshooting.			
POSITION	**BIOMECHANICAL ACTION**	**VERBAL CUES**	**ERRORS**	**CAUSES OF ERRORS**
Post	■ Play slightly back on ball side of post player when he/she is 15 feet or farther from basket ■ Wave near hand to discourage pass ■ If post player is 10 to 15 feet from the basket, move in close to player by keeping the hand and foot nearest the ball between him/her and the ball while the opposite foot and hand are kept between your opponent and the basket ■ Watch for lob pass to weak side ■ Keep moving to maintain position ■ If post player goes outside, sag back into lane to help teammates ■ Block off or screen opponent from getting rebound after a shot ■ Open up if screener comes over	■ Play ball side of opponent ■ Wave hands ■ Split opponent up close if within 15 feet of basket ■ Keep moving	1. Allow post player to receive ball near basket	1. Post player sets up first and defender plays behind 2. Didn't open up on screen
Wing player	■ Consider the distance of opponent from ball and basket ■ If close to the ball, play even with the wing so you can see both player and ball ■ Close in with near hand up, thumb down, to discourage pass	■ Play close when near ball ■ Drift toward lane away from ball ■ Play even with wing, hands up	1. Wing receives ball near basket	1. Lost visual contact with offensive player; poor defensive positioning; poor balance in stance

(continued)

TABLE 3.19 Continued.

POSITION	BIOMECHANICAL ACTION	VERBAL CUES	ERRORS	CAUSES OF ERRORS
	■ Back foot and other hand should be between wing and basket ■ If wing is away from the ball, move away from player toward lane area ■ Keep vision on both player and ball	■ Be able to see ball and player		
Guard	■ Drift back toward lane area ■ Point one hand toward player and other toward the ball ■ Maintain vision of ball and opponent ■ Block path toward basket if opponent becomes a cutter	■ Drift to lane ■ Point: player—ball ■ See ball and player ■ Keep moving	1. Guard receives ball near basket	1. Lost visual contact with offensive player; poor positioning

Guard a pivot player on the side, a little to the front

Figure 3.96
Guarding a post player.

Three-on-two situations are similar to two-on-one situations, but having two defenders requires the defense to coordinate its movements for efficient, effective play. Generally, one defensive player positions just above the foul line, and the other is in the lane just in front of the basket. The front player's responsibility is to stop the ball above the foul circle, if possible. When the ball stops or is passed, the front player opens up toward the direction of the ball but slides toward the cutter on the opposite side. The front player is still responsible for the middle player (original passer); he/she must be ready to cover two players.

The back player takes the cutter who receives the first pass and must not allow this cutter to get an easy basket. The longer the offense takes to attempt to score, the more likely it is that help will arrive in time to set up the team defense.

Four-on-three and other outnumbered defensive situations require hustle and an attempt to get the offense to make several passes to slow down the attack. Verbal communication among the defensive players will help identify who is going to cover whom. Generally, the defense should try to cover an area (zone) and help each other as much as possible.

Individual Defense Drills

Defense is best taught within the framework of team play and the coordination of players to offer support and to help to make the defensive efforts as effective as possible. The following drills are suggested to help teach individual defensive fundamentals and to begin to introduce team defense. More team-oriented defensive strategies will be discussed in Section 4. Drills #62 and #63 are designed specifically to teach the defensive stance, how to maintain this position during movement, and how to slide the feet without crossing over.

Drill #62: Defensive Slide Drill

In Figure 3.97a the players begin the Defensive Slide Drill by taking a defensive stance and slide laterally. At each junction of lines, they change direction but continue the lateral defensive sliding movement. The next player in line waits until the player in front of him/her comes to the first junction before starting to slide.

The players slide laterally to junction 1, retreat steps to junction 2, slide laterally to junction 5, approach steps to junction 6, slide laterally to junction 7, retreat steps to junction 8, slide laterally to junction 9, retreat steps to junction 10, slide laterally to junction 11, retreat steps to junction 12, and slide laterally to junction 13 and the finish (see 3.98b).

CUES:
1. Keep head and chin up
2. Bend knees; keep hips and buttocks low
3. Back straight
4. Slide feet

Drill #63: Towel Drill

In the Towel Drill, the players pair up in four alleys according to the most desirable match-ups. Pairs can be by position, by speed and quickness, or perhaps a big, slow player paired with a quick little player. The defensive player assumes a stance with one leg slightly ahead of the other. The head should be the midway point between the spread of the legs and should act as a balance to prevent body weight from being shifted too much on one leg. Players also must begin and remain in a low position throughout the drill. This is effected by using a "tugging" towel held across the back of the neck.

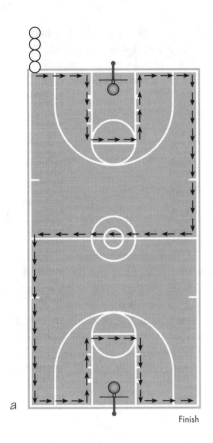
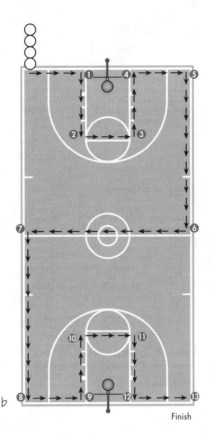

Figure 3.97
Defensive slide drill.

Figure 3.98
Towel drill.

This drill should attempt to impart only two defensive principles that enable the defense to beat the offense:

1. Beat the dribbler to a line and force him/her to change direction,
2. Play the ball tough when he's/she's forced to use a cross-over dribble in changing direction.

The players are taught to slide their feet (no hopping), and how to shift their feet in changing direction. The dribbler follows an angular course as shown in Figure 3.98. This should resemble beating the defense via the baseline or sideline; when cut off at a line, he/she must cross-over dribble, change direction, and try to beat the defense via another "line." Dribbling techniques of keeping the ball low, keeping the body poised, protecting the ball, and change-of-pace or decoy dribbling should be stressed.

CUES: 1. Keep hips and buttocks low
2. Spread feet
3. Slide

The next group of drills is designed to consider positioning, guarding the ball handler, playing defense against an offensive player without the ball, and defensing the shooter under various conditions.

Drill #64: One-on-One Half-court Drill

In the One-on-One Drill (Figure 3.99), the players pair up according to position they are likely to play, and work one-on-one. Two or three pairs are at a basket, with only one pair working at a time.

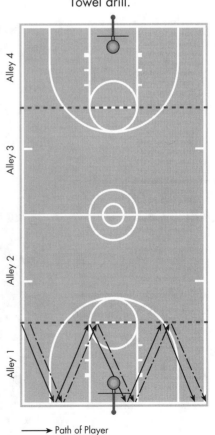

Figure 3.99

One-on-one half-court drill.

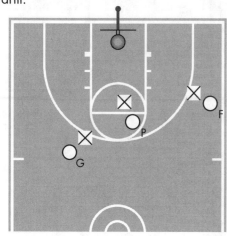

back door *a cut along the baseline when a player is being overplayed by the defense or when the defense turns to look at the ball*

This can be a competitive drill encompassing different scoring conditions. One idea: An offensive foul counts 2 points for the defensive player; a steal is 2 points. The objective is to see how many points the defense can score when the offense has possession of the ball five times.

CUES: 1. Slide
2. Focus on midsection
3. Hand in face
4. Go straight up

Drill #65: Wing Adjustment Drill

The Wing Adjustment Drill (Figure 3.100) is a two-person defensive drill designed to work on defensive positioning of the two wings. Depending on where the ball is located, the two defensive players must move accordingly. With the ball on the top left side of Player 1, X_1 is in a denial position, preventing O_2 from receiving the ball. X_2 is in a help position to stop the **back door** pass. If O_1 passes the ball to O_3, X_2 now moves to a denial position while X_1 takes a help position. In this drill the ball is reversed back and forth so that the two defensive players really have to work on denying and then quickly getting in the help position.

CUES: 1. Play close, near ball
2. Drift toward lane away from ball
3. Play even with wing, hand up
4. See ball and player

Drills #66 and #67 add defensive players to create more team movement and positioning and more game-like situations.

Drill #66: Deny Drill

The purpose of the Deny Drill, shown in Figure 3.101, is to deny the ball to the offense. The defensive player must always stay between his/her opponent and the ball. Two coaches/teachers are part of the offense. They pass the ball to each

Figure 3.100 (on left)

Wing adjustment drill.

Figure 3.101 (on right)

Deny drill.

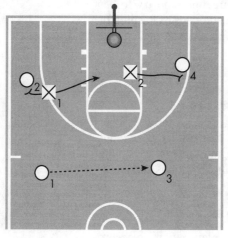

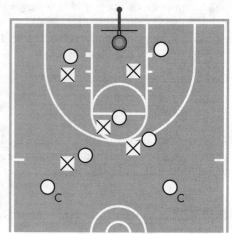

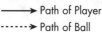
→ Path of Player
┄┄► Path of Ball

other, and they pass to the offense, which in turn tries to score. The coaches/teachers may move to various positions on the floor (there is no defense on the coaches). The players can stay on offense as long as they score. The defense must take the ball away from the offense. Penalties should be assessed for scoring or offensive rebounding.

CUES: 1. See ball and player
2. Play ball side of opponent
3. Drift to lane if ball is away

Drill #67: Competitive Shell Drill

The Competitive Shell Drill (Figure 3.102) is a man-to-man defensive drill in a game-type situation. The game is played four-on-four in the half court. Play begins with (a) a dribble across the half court line or (b) a throw-in from out-of-bounds. Teams X and O have the ball for five possessions with one point given to the defensive team for each basket the offense scores. Fouls and violations are called by the coach/teacher. The team accumulating the fewest points wins. To encourage players to take charging fouls, the defense has a point subtracted from their score for each charging foul called.

CUES: 1. Good stance
2. See ball and player
3. Keep moving

To practice defense when outnumbered, Drill #57, Two-on-One, and Drill #58, Three-on-Two, Two-on-One Break can be used. The focus, however, is on the defensive play. Cues for each drill correspond to the cues presented previously.

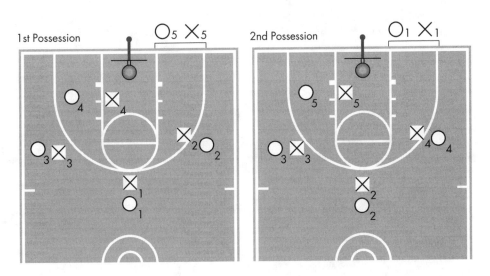

Figure 3.102
Competitive shell drill.

Strategies

Strategy is an important component in any game or sport. In basketball, the ability of one team to control the tempo or pace of the game affects the outcome of the game. The idea is to get the opponent to play the way you want to play. If you can get your opponent to play to your strengths, you will have a greater opportunity to win.

Basketball is a fast-paced and complex game in which any number of different team offenses and defenses may be utilized to help one team gain an advantage over the opponent. The seemingly endless variety of team strategies employed in today's game of basketball mandates that every team be drilled and prepared to counter or control the events on the court. In this section we will examine what is necessary for successful preparation and play of this wonderful game of basketball.

First, we will examine the psychological strategies to enhance performance. The mental preparation needed to play basketball successfully must include concentration, visualization, and relaxation strategies.

Next we will cover game strategies for team offensive play, team defensive play, anticipating opponents' strategies, and adjusting to specific individual characteristics of opponents.

PREVIEW OF STRATEGIES

1. Psychological Strategies to Enhance Performance
   A. Concentration
   B. Visualization
   C. Relaxation
      1. progressive relaxation
      2. breath control
2. Game/Activity Strategies
   A. Team offense
      1. offensive principles
      2. types of offenses

a. man-to-man variations

b. zone

c. press

d. fast break

e. out-of-bounds

B. Team defense

1. defense principles

2. types of defenses:

a. man-to-man

b. zone

c. stopping the break

C. Anticipating opponent's strategies

1. scouting: team

2. time-outs

D. Adjusting to characteristics of opponents

1. scouting: individual players

2. substituting

PSYCHOLOGICAL STRATEGIES TO ENHANCE PERFORMANCE

concentration the ability to keep focused on relevant environment cues

Concentration

Concentration is the ability to maintain focus on relevant environment cues (Weinberg & Gould, 1995). Relevant environmental cues refers to a player focusing on actions that are part of a skill, strategy, or the game that will help the player perform. The following example might help answer the question, "What cues in a basketball player's environment are relevant or irrelevant?"

> A basketball player is shooting two free throws at the end of a game with only a couple of seconds left and his/her team down by one point. A relevant cue might be making sure he/she goes through his/her normal pre-shot routine— bouncing the ball three times, taking a deep breath, looking up at the basket, and focusing on the front of the rim. Irrelevant cues include the players lined up for the rebound and the hometown fans behind the backboard waving their hands and making a lot of noise. (Weinberg & Gould, 1995, p. 334)

The player who can focus on the pre-shot routine while eliminating all extraneous noise and movements will have a much better chance of successfully executing the foul shot.

Concentration requires more than focusing on relevant environmental cues. It also encompasses the ability to maintain attention throughout the duration of a game. Maintaining focus over long periods is not easy. One factor is fatigue. Fatigue affects concentration because the performer can be easily distracted by irrelevant cues such as muscle soreness, heavy breathing, and perspiration.

Other distractions include one's thoughts, other events, and emotions. Attending to past events or not being able to forget about what just happened often causes a loss of concentration. A bad call, a mistake, or a fluke event often keeps players from focusing on the present.

Attending to future events also can cause a player to lose concentration. Examples are, "What if we lose the game?" and "What if I make another error?" This future-oriented thinking and worry impedes concentration.

Another potential concentration breaker is attending to too many cues. Sometimes the player wants to impress someone in the audience and tries to perform beyond his/her capabilities. This player is concentrating on cues that aren't helping his/her performance. The keys to concentration, therefore, are to focus on only the *relevant cues* in the athletic environment and to *eliminate distractions*.

To help the basketball player improve his/her concentration for the duration of a game:

1. Practice with distractions such as a noisy gym or in a gym that is extremely hot in anticipation of game conditions on an opponent's home court.

2. Use cue words to trigger a particular response. The free throw shooter may think: relax, set free, focus on target, extend knees and legs, reach for the basket.

3. Establish routines to help eliminate distractions and structure the time before performance and between performances so the player can focus when it's time to perform.

4. Stay focused in the present. Beware of thinking in the past and future. Maintain focus on what is happening *now*.

Visualization

Mental rehearsal of sport performance is becoming an important element of training for many athletes. **Imagery** involves recalling from memory pieces of information stored from experience and then shaping these pieces into meaningful images (Weinberg & Gould, 1995). Through imagery, an athlete can re-create previous positive experiences or picture new events to prepare for performance. Thus, imagined events can affect the nervous system, and the brain, identical to actual experiences.

imagery *creating or re-creating an experience in the mind*

Although imagery is often called "visualization," the kinesthetic, auditory, tactile, and olfactory senses also are utilized to re-create performance or create new events. Various theories suggest that imagery works by producing muscle activity, by providing a mental blueprint, or by improving psychological skills such as concentration, confidence, and control of emotional responses.

Imagery requires practice. Vivid images are important to successful creation and re-creation. The closer the images are to real experience, the better the transfer to actual performance. The athlete should pay attention to details such as type of court, closeness of spectators, and temperature of the facility. Also, emotions and thoughts from actual competition, such as anxiety, concentration, or exhilaration, can help make imagined performance seem more real.

Relaxation

Anxiety plays a large role in basketball performance. *State anxiety* is a conscious feeling of apprehension and tension stemming mainly from the individual's perception of the present or upcoming situation as threatening.

anxiety *a negatively charged emotional state characterized by internal discomfort and a feeling of nervousness*

Arousal, which is often confused with anxiety, is a part of sports performance. Excessive anxiety can diminish performance. It can produce muscle tension, which may cause a player's movements to be rigid or awkward. Optimal arousal, on the other hand, helps a player perform at his/her best. If a player's level of arousal is too low or too high, performance may suffer. The optimum point of arousal varies as a function of task characteristics; therefore, different sports tasks are likely to demand different levels of arousal for the best results.

arousal *the intensity of behavior on a continuum from sleep to extensive excitement*

Sport psychologists have been applying relaxation techniques to sport and exercise situations in an effort to help athletes and performers control their emotions and counter the negative performance effects of anxiety and less than optimal arousal.

Progressive Relaxation

progressive relaxation
a relaxation technique
that involves tensing and
relaxing specific muscles
sequentially

Progressive relaxation, sometimes referred to as *muscle relaxation* (Jacobson, 1938), is a relaxation technique based on the premise that one can learn the difference between tension and relaxation. It is not possible to be relaxed and tense at the same time. Thus, by systematically contracting and relaxing each major muscle group in the body, one can relax the body by decreasing muscle tension, which in turn will decrease mental tension or the negative effects of anxiety or improper arousal.

Breath Control

breath control a
relaxation technique that
involves proper breathing
to control anxiety and
muscle tension

Another technique that enables an individual to relax is **breath control.** Proper breathing may be the easiest way to control anxiety and muscle tension. When under pressure, the breathing is short, shallow, and irregular. Basketball is filled with pressure situations that can interfere with breathing and proper performance. Research has demonstrated that holding the breath increases muscle tension and breathing out decreases tension. In pressure situations, many players unconsciously hold their breath, which causes performance problems.

Breath control can be developed by learning to breathe from the diaphragm instead of the chest. Slowly inhaling and exhaling can help the player maintain his/her composure and control over anxiety during stressful times.

The following suggestions may help basketball players relax prior to competition.

1. *Release stress through physical activity.* The pre-game warm-up gives players a chance to turn thought-induced stress into physical stress, which may help the players relax or combat anxiety.
2. *Promote task familiarity.* Again during pre-game warm-ups, the routine (activities or tasks) should be one with which the players are comfortable and have rehearsed many times. Other routines, such as eating times, meetings, or quiet times, should also follow a set format or routine that allows the players to feel confident and in control.
3. *Practice stressful situations.* During practice sessions rehearse the skills and strategies that will be used in competition until they are mastered.
4. *Build self-confidence.* By preparing game plans, or by reviewing a player's strengths, an opponent's weaknesses, and team strategies, a player can gain confidence about an upcoming contest and reduce the threatening feeling that uncertainty can create in one's mind.

The successful basketball player controls his/her emotions during activity or competition. The following relaxation techniques can be applied to contest-specific situations.

1. *Practice breath control.* Use breath control during time-outs, while preparing for a free throw, during a substitution, or any other break in the player's game action. Breath control can help the player focus on breathing and not on environmental distractions such as crowd or opponent antics.
2. *Keep errors in perspective.* The player should strive to stay focused on the present. Worrying about one's mistakes during competition can increase anxiety and hinder performance.
3. *Avoid self-focusing.* Negative thinking can make anxiety more acute. Players should focus on tasks at hand and expect favorable outcomes.
4. *Slow down, take your time, and have fun.* Legendary UCLA Coach John Wooden said, "Be quick, but don't hurry." Though he applied this phrase to many basketball situations, here it seems appropriate to remind the player that

performing hurriedly and haphazardly often leads to errors and muscle tension. This can lead to negative performance, and the "fun" is lost from the play. Players should look forward to challenges and avoid the tendency to rush through their responsibilities.

GAME/ACTIVITY STRATEGIES: TEAM OFFENSE

Successful team offense is characterized by unselfish, intelligent, and effortful play by each team member. I believe that the best way to teach and instill positive team qualities is to drill players properly in execution of the fundamentals. By developing the fundamentals thoroughly, players begin to learn how to make quick decisions and adjustments in a constantly changing game. They will better understand their strengths and weaknesses, which can facilitate unselfish play, as well as understanding of the roles they are best suited for to make a positive contribution to their team. By establishing positive work and play habits in developing their fundamentals, players will begin to appreciate what type of effort is required to successfully execute optimal play.

Principles of Sound Offense

Several principles are involved in becoming a sound offensive team. First and foremost is the aforementioned development of the fundamental skills of basketball. Second is keeping the floor balanced or providing sufficient spacing to create operating room for the player with the ball. Generally, 15-foot spacing between players is required. This balance or spacing allows for the efficient movement of the ball and players. The ball must be moved quickly from player to player to keep the defense from concentrating around the basket. In addition, player movement keeps the defense "honest," forcing the players to consider each offensive player as a threat to the defense.

The primary objective for offensive play is to create good scoring opportunities. While floor balance helps force the defense to play each offensive player equally, the offense must keep the defense occupied "on the ball" and "away from the ball." "Playing without the ball" is a fundamental skill stressed in individual offense and, therefore, a primary principle of team offense. This **weak-side play** must be emphasized as much as **strong-side play.** Weak-side offensive play is so important because if the defense does not respect or play the weak-side, the defense will have an advantage by either **trapping** the ball or congesting the basket area.

A sound offense also provides strong offensive rebound position on all shots. Again, floor balance is a key for this rebound position to be established. The offense should force the defense to commit itself to stopping any option the offense is executing. The offense then can exploit the defense by attacking an opening that any defense adjustments create to stop the first option.

An additional principle is that a sound offense must provide good defensive balance. This refers to the team's ability to make the transition from offense to defense quickly and efficiently so the opponent will not have an advantage. John Wooden, renowned coach of the UCLA Bruins, sums up floor balance and good offensive principles:

> I like the floor balance to usually provide a strong-side cut, a weak-side cut, a cut across the top of the key, triangular rebounding power underneath, a man in the foul circle area to cover long rebounds, and a protector. (Wooden, 1966, p. 137)

The principles of a sound offense, in sum, are the following.

1. Provide proper floor spacing or a balanced floor with 15-foot spacing between players.

weak-side play play on the side of the court away from the ball
strong-side play play on the side of the court where the ball is currently located
trapping a defensive tactic wherein two or more defenders surround the ball to block passing lanes and to take away driving or shooting opportunities for the offense

2. Keep the defense occupied both "on the ball" and "on the weak-side."
3. Provide strong offensive rebound position.
4. Force the defense to commit itself to stopping any option the offense is executing.
5. Provide defensive balance.
6. Recognize favorable offensive opportunities (such as open shots and blocks).

Types of Offense

Most basketball teachers and coaches believe that good execution of offense is more than the selection of any particular offense. Players must know and understand what to expect while executing a particular offense. Therefore, the offensive fundamental drills should reflect the offense so players can see the relationship between the drills and offensive play. In addition, the progression of the drills and the number of players used in the drills should be sequential until a five-player team functions as a unit.

The specific offenses presented in this section are the passing or motion game and zone offenses. Also, the single-post offense and the triple-post offense will be examined briefly.

SKILL 1   Man-to-Man Offensive Variations

Passing or Motion Game (offense)

The passing game is the focal offense for this book because it is not a set play offense. This offense emphasizes movement of the ball, movement of personnel, shot selection, and team play. Set rules are applied to constant movement of all five players that takes them to all five positions on the court. The rules will be taught to enable the offense to take advantage of opportunities the defense presents. This is an offense based on recognizing what the defense is doing (where its players are positioned), then reacting to offensively take advantage of the situation. This offense also is presented because:

- It is easy to teach
- It can be run from any initial formation
- It develops team play
- It improves team ball handling
- It allows for good offensive rebounding
- It teaches players how to play offensive basketball.

The primary objective of the passing or motion game is to get a good shot—defined as a shot that is within a player's shooting ability, one in which the defensive pressure is minimal, and one that has teammates in good rebounding position. The three primary fundamentals in obtaining good shots through the motion offense are *passing, cutting,* and *screening.* Not all players have the same shooting or scoring ability. Therefore, each player must know and recognize shooting and scoring opportunities best suited to his/her abilities.

Fundamentally, all five players must be good passers. All passes should be sharp and crisp. The most important element in passing is to pass *away* from the defensive player instead of passing to the offensive player. Also, the amount of dribbling should be minimal, if not totally eliminated.

Cutting can either be a move to get away from the defensive player or to set up a screen by a teammate. A **"V" cut,** or the action of taking the defensive player in the direction he/she is playing and then utilizing the "V" concept to cut opposite

"V" cut *an offensive action that takes the defense in the direction it is playing and then cutting opposite the ball or shot*

for the ball or shot is important. Almost all of the cutting action to get the shot takes place away from the ball.

Constant movement of the players and the ball should ultimately result in a good shot. By adding screening to the movement, the defense will have to make decisions or adjustments that make these tasks more difficult and the shots freer. The most effective use of screening with the motion offense can be made away from the ball. Effective use of a screen is dependent upon the action of both the screener and the cutter. The screener has to read the position of the defensive player that is going to be screened to enable the cutter to make maximum use of the screen. The action of screening is an example of team basketball, in which two and sometimes three players work together to help one player get open for a good shot. The following discussion will look at three types of screens, the basic "pick and roll" play, and drills that can be utilized to teach screening and how to use the screen.

Screening

An offensive player(s) uses **screening** to temporarily interrupt the movement of a defensive player. The screener stands in a position such that the opposing defensive player cannot get to the player in position to shoot. Also, players moving without the ball can use a screen to free themselves or to set a screen to free a teammate.

Three types of screens are lateral set screen, baseline jam, and rear screen, diagrammed in Figures 4.1, 4.2, and 4.3.

CUES 1. Set screen on side of defender
          2. Feet parallel, shoulder-width apart, knees flexed, stationary
          3. Screener pops backward toward ball
          4. If defense switches, roll to the basket or the ball

CUES 1. Set screen along baseline
          2. Feet parallel, shoulder-width apart, knees flexed, stationary

CUES 1. Set screen behind defender
          2. Feet parallel, shoulder-width apart, knees flexed, stationary
          3. Set screen (stop) distance equivalent of one step from defender

Setting a screen and using a screen require constant attention throughout a drill. Screening and using a screen can be, and should be, practiced in combination with other fundamental skills such as passing, dribbling, and shooting. Figure 4.4 depicts screening and using screen drills in the Pick and Roll.

screening (or pick) a maneuver used by an offensive player who, without causing contact, delays or prevents an opponent from reaching a desired position

Figure 4.1 (on left)
Lateral screen ("screen away").

Figure 4.2 (center)
Baseline screen ("down screen").

Figure 4.3 (on right)
Rear screen ("back screen").

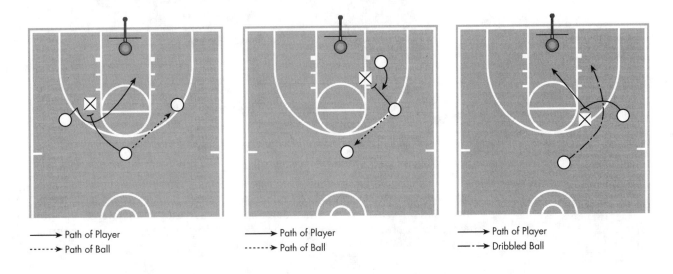

→ Path of Player	→ Path of Player	→ Path of Player
----→ Path of Ball	----→ Path of Ball	—·→ Dribbled Ball

Figure 4.4

Screening in the pick and roll.

Offensive player (white shirt) dribbles off screener, forcing defender (black shirt) into screen

Defensive player steps out, blocking path to basket and/or taking away jump shot from offensive player. When screener feels contact from defensive player, he does a reverse pivot and cuts to basket. Offensive player throws a pass to screener.

Screening Drills

Drill #68: Open Up Early Backdoor

The Open Up Early Backdoor Drill (Figure 4.5) is effective against a switching player defense. Set up O₁ in a guard position and O₂ in a wing position, with X's playing defense. Player O₂ sets a pick, and O₁ begins to dribble toward him/her. Before O₁ reaches the pick, O₂ opens up and goes to the basket for a pass from O₁.

VARIATIONS:

1. Do this drill with a high post player and guard.
2. Do this drill with two guards.

CUES 1. Set screen on side of defender
2. Roll to basket

Drill #69: Pass and Screen Away Drill

In the Pass and Screen Away Drill (Figure 4.6), Players O₂ and O₃ are in the wing position, and O₁ is at the point. Player O₁ passes to O₂ and screens away to O₃ (a). Player O₃ has following options:

1. Replace O₁ on top
2. Curl and go to the basket.
3. Backdoor and go to the basket.

Player O₂ passes to O₃, utilizing any of these three moves (b).

CUES: 1. O₃—shuffle cut
2. O₁—set screen on side of defender

Drill #70: Screen Down and Across Drill

For the Screen Down and Across Drill (Figure 4.7), set up Players O₁ and O₂ in a stack, with O₃ at the opposite low post and O with the ball on top. Player O₂ screens down for O₁, who pops out to wing, and O₂ continues across baseline to

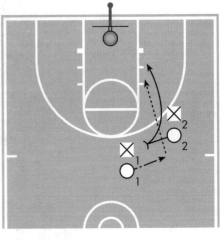

Figure 4.5
Open up early backdoor drill.

———▶ Path of Player
------▶ Passed Ball
—-—▶ Dribbled Ball

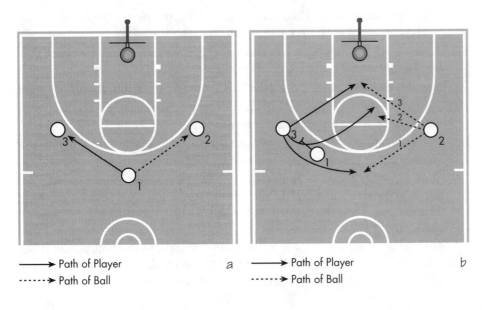

———▶ Path of Player   *a*
------▶ Path of Ball

———▶ Path of Player   *b*
------▶ Path of Ball

Figure 4.6
Pass and screen away drill.

Figure 4.7

Screen down and across drill.

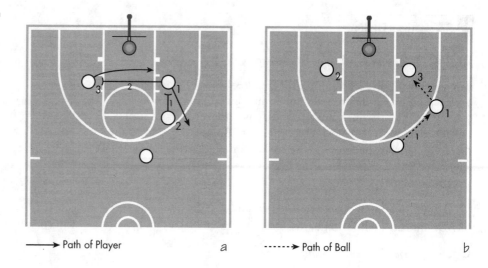

→ Path of Player   *a*   ·····▸ Path of Ball   *b*

screen for O3, who flashes to the ball side, low post (a). Then O passes to O1, who passes in low to O3 (b).

VARIATIONS:

1. Set up a man defense and run the drill.
2. Have Player O2 flash high to the ball side as an option.

CUES: 1. Lateral set
2. Baseline jam screen
3. Shuffle cut

Rules of the Passing Game

The following rules serve as guidelines to movement of the players and balance of the offense.

1. *After making a pass, move. The three options are:*
   a. Go set a screen for a perimeter player to cut toward the ball or basket.
   b. Cut to the basket looking for a return pass.
   c. Go set a screen on the ball but only after *three* passes have been made. Any player, not just the passer, can screen on the ball.
2. *Always make the easy pass, and make a minimum of three passes on each possession,* unless a lay-up presents itself sooner.
3. *Look to pass first, shoot second, and drive third, in the* **triple-threat position.**
4. **Split-the-post.** Any time the ball goes inside to a player posting up, the passer will screen the nearest perimeter player to scissors off the post.
5. *Post up.* Only players assigned to the best post players can at any time break across the lane toward the ball and post up for a pass.
6. *Upon receiving a pass, face the basket for a count of two.* This will allow for things to develop and allow the player with the ball to see where it should go. This also will allow the player with the ball to assume the triple-threat position and keep the defense honest.
7. *Use the dribble.* The dribble is necessary to advance the ball up court but should be minimized or eliminated against a man-to-man defense. In the front court, use the dribble in the following two situations:

triple-threat position
holding the ball near the hip so the player can pass, shoot, or drive

split-the-post a three-player offensive maneuver in which the ball is passed to a post player and two players then scissor-off this post player for a possible pass

a. Drive to the basket when the opportunity presents itself.

b. Use the dribble to improve the passing angle.

8. *Perimeter rules.*

a. After making a pass inside to a **post player,** slide toward the baseline looking for a return pass and shot. *Or,* split the post by screening for another perimeter player to cut toward the ball. Perimeter players must be feeders first and shooters second. Get the ball into the post players by playing slow and waiting for things to happen inside.

b. After making a pass to a **perimeter player,** go set a screen for a perimeter player to cut toward the ball or basket. Other possibilities include replacing yourself or releasing back to the ball, especially if the defense switches; screening on the ball; or cutting to the basket looking for a return pass.

c. *If the wing cuts over the top* of the screen set *by the point,* the screener always will continue movement to the baseline and cross the lane to the other side, looking to set a screen or use a screen.

d. Any time the *wing goes below the screen set by the point,* the screener must replace himself/herself at the point and the wing cuts through the low post area, continuing out to the perimeter.

9. *Post rules.*

a. As a *high post,* whenever you have *not* received the ball after two counts of posting up, move diagonally across the lane to screen for the other post player *or* slide down the lane on ball side to the low post area to post up.

b. As a *low post,* whenever you have not received the ball after two counts of posting up, clear to the opposite side of the lane and set a lateral screen if the other post player is in the area.

c. Both post players should stay close to the lane unless a perimeter player is having trouble making a pass. In this case, either post can go outside to get a pass.

post player *a pivot player stationed near the basket and facing away from it*

perimeter player *a player stationed around the outer boundaries of the lane who feeds and shoots the ball*

Basic Formations for the Passing Game

Another reason for teaching the passing game is that it can be started from virtually any set or formation. This will allow teams to use formations that best utilize the different abilities of their players and take advantage of the teams' offensive strengths. Figures 4.8 and 4.9 illustrate the variety of formations from which the motion (passing) game can be initiated.

Figure 4.10 illustrates one basic formation (double low) to begin the high/low passing game.

The point guard (1) must declare a side of the floor. The baseline player (3) has two choices—an outside cut or cross the lane and screen. Players 2 and 4 will delay their initial cuts until the pass from 1 is being released. Players 4 and 5, the post players, will always break high to the free throw line. The offside baseline player (2) has the options of breaking out high or looping around Player 4 and cutting toward the opposite corner.

After the baseline cross and screen is completed, the options with the ball at the wing or high post remain the same (Figure 4.11). This is the movement if Player 2 loops around Player 4 and cuts across the lane to the corner to begin the offense.

Perimeter movement is depicted in Figure 4.12. (a) The screener at the wing will always continue his/her movement to the baseline and then cross the lane. If he/she doesn't receive a screen or pass, he/she can fill a wing or return to the original side of the floor. (b) Upon making the pass, the wing will set a screen for any-

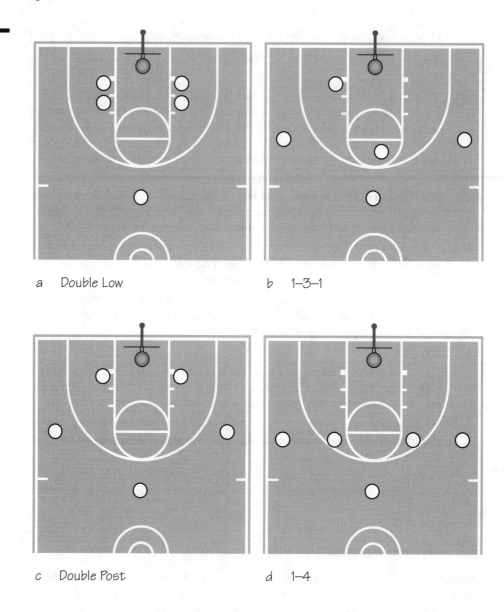

Figure 4.8
High-low passing game formation.

a   Double Low

b   1–3–1

c   Double Post

d   1–4

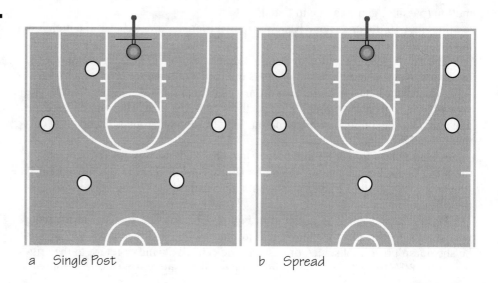

Figure 4.9
Single post and no post formations.

a   Single Post

b   Spread

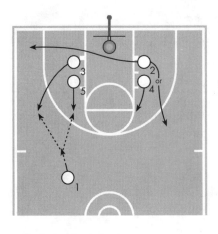

a   Outside Cut

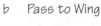

b   Pass to Wing

Figure 4.10
Basic set used to get into high/low passing game.

⟶ Path of Player
⤑ Passed Ball
⟶ Dribbled Ball

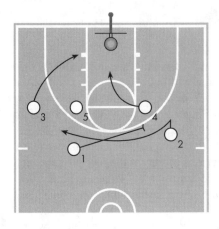

c   Pass to Post

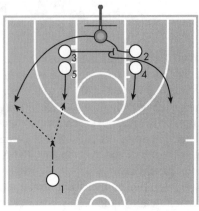

d   Cross and screen

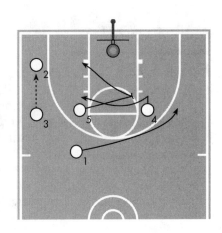

Figure 4.11
Basic options in high/low post passing game.

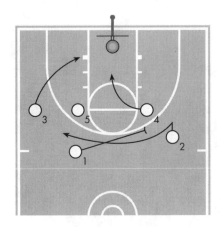

a   Basic Movement

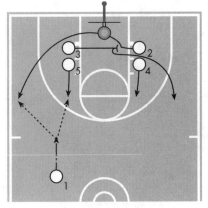

b   Perimeter to Post Pass

The low post player (5) *must* clear to the opposite side of the lane for this play to work.

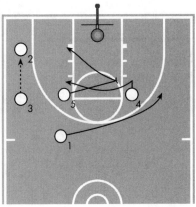

c   High Post Screen on the Ball

Any time the ball goes to a post player, the perimeter players use this type of scissors action.

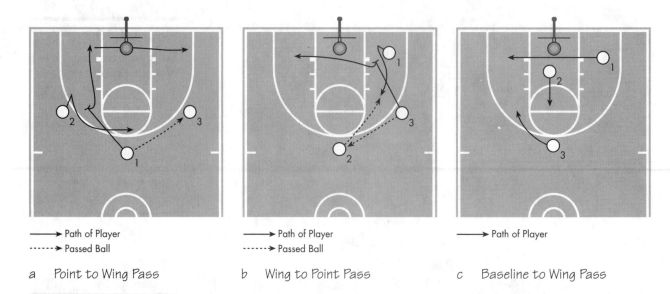

→ Path of Player
---→ Passed Ball

→ Path of Player
---→ Passed Ball

→ Path of Player

a   Point to Wing Pass   b   Wing to Point Pass   c   Baseline to Wing Pass

Figure 4.12
Perimeter movement.

one on the baseline, and then cross the lane. With the ball, the point always can pass the ball inside to a post or drive to the side without a wing player. (c) After making the pass, Player 3 crosses to the other side of the floor toward the baseline.

Figure 4.13 depicts post movement. (a) If Player 5 can't receive the pass after posting up at the high-post area for two seconds, he/she goes diagonally to screen for Player 4. The low post cuts off the screen to the high post. Player 5 must release back toward the ball and post up low. (b) After posting up at the low post and not receiving a pass, Player 5 will cross the lane to set a lateral screen if Player 4 is there. Normally, Player 4 will want to cut off the screen toward the baseline side so Player 5 can release to the high-post area.

The passing or motion game offense requires constant attention. The most effective way to teach this offense is by playing five-on-five. This will help players develop timing, cohesion, and floor spacing while allowing for all positions to develop together. In teaching the offense, the situations or rules can be modified to develop concepts or emphasize specific passing game rules. Some modification examples are:

1. No dribbling allowed, only passing. This teaches player movement and ball handling.

Figure 4.13
Post movements.

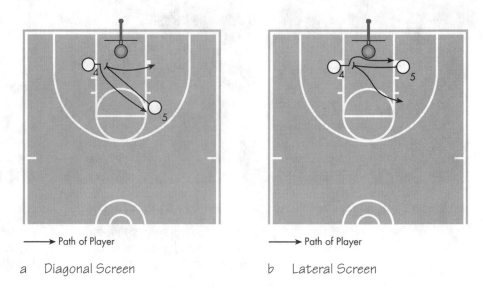

→ Path of Player

→ Path of Player

a   Diagonal Screen   b   Lateral Screen

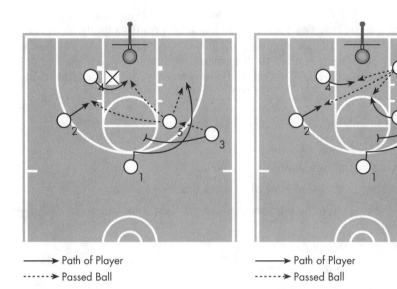

Figure 4.13
Continued.

———➤ Path of Player
------➤ Passed Ball

———➤ Path of Player
------➤ Passed Ball

c   High-Post Pass Options

d   High-Post Pass Option

2. Shots may be taken only in the lane. This encourages passes into the post and good high/low post play.

3. Shots may be taken only if there has been a specific screen set (low-post off-ball screen, rear screen away from ball, or a screen on the ball, for example).

4. Set the number of passes to be made before a shot can be taken (such as a minimum of three passes up to 10 or 12). This encourages patience, ball handling, and decision making.

5. Perimeter player drills and post player drills can be broken down to emphasize specific situations or conditions, but five-on-five drills should remain the focal point of the instruction.

Single-Post Offense

The basic positioning for a single-post offense is to have the post player at the free throw line as pictured in Figure 4.14, with two guards and wings on each side of the lane (a) or by having the post start low (b).

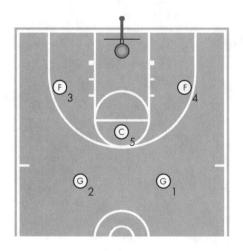

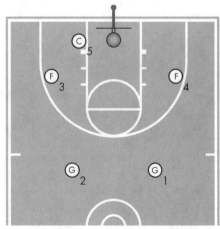

Figure 4.14
Basic positioning for a single-post offense.

a   Two guards and wings

b   Post starts low

The single-post offense has been utilized in many ways through the years. Although John Wooden's UCLA single-post offense is perhaps the most famous, many variations have been applied to this basic formation. The *flex offense,* described below, is one example. This offense, also known as the **spots offense,** offers the following advantages:

1. assigned safety players—one or two
2. designated shooters and rebounders
3. can be used as a controlled offense—slow tempo
4. can be used as an "early" offense off the fast break—fast tempo
5. a variety of entries into the offense gives it a different look and makes it difficult to defense

   Example: guard-to-guard entry

   guard-to-forward entry

   guard-to-center entry
6. any player can start the offense

   Example: a small center could start the offense
   against pressure
7. small teams as well as big power teams can use this offense
8. only four basic moves in the offense keep this offense simple, allowing more work on techniques
9. constant movement by all players—every time a pass is made, all players move according to the position they are in at the time

The spots offense received its name from the idea that five major spots on the floor must be filled at all times while the offense is in operation. Figure 4.15 identifies the five major spots. Notice that Player 5 has to be at the low post on either side of the lane.

The offense has only four basic moves:

1. Guard position: Any time guard passes the ball to opposite guard, screen down and remain there until next pass is made (Figure 4.16).

spots offense the five major spots on the court that are filled all the time during operation of offense

Figure 4.15 (on left)
Major spots in flex offense.

Figure 4.16 (on right)
Guard position in spots offense.

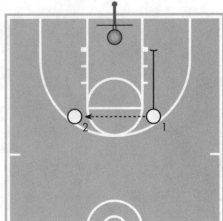

2. The #5 spot: Wait for screen and go high to the spot where the player who screened for you came from (Figure 4.17).

3. Strong side forward (forward on same side as low post player (Figure 4.18): (a) Wait for guard on side to pass away from him/her to opposite guard and then (b) shuffle-cut off low post and become low post on opposite side.

4. Weak side forward (forward on side away from low post (Figure 4.19): Any time you find yourself in the forward position away from the low post, immediately "flair" out away, opening up the middle for the cutter. Be ready to be the next cutter on the next pass away from him/her.

The basic offense set (Figure 4.20) can be started on either side of the lane from either the #1 or #2 spots. The #1 point guard brings ball into play (a) while #2 off guard sets a screen for weak side forward #3, who steps inside, then breaks up into the #2 spot. Player #1 passes the ball to #3, (b), then sets the screen for the #5 low-post player; #3, when he/she catches the ball, squares up to the basket, and looks for his/her shot, then looks inside to #4 cutting off low post. If Player #4 is not open, the pass is made across to #5 breaking high (c) and sequence is continued.

Passing is stressed, as it is in the passing game or motion offense. The ball should be dribbled only as follows:

1. as an entry into the offense

2. to improve the passing angle

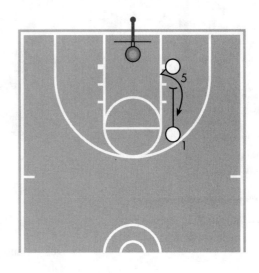

Figure 4.17
Waiting for screen and going high.

⟶ Path of Player

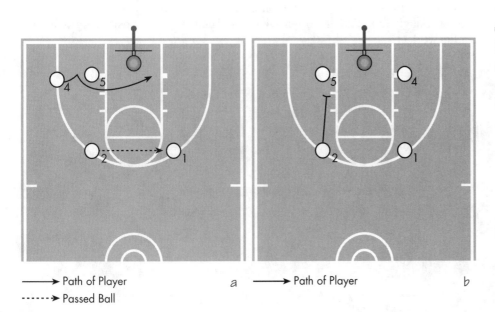

⟶ Path of Player
- - - -▶ Passed Ball

a

⟶ Path of Player

b

Figure 4.18
Strong side forward.

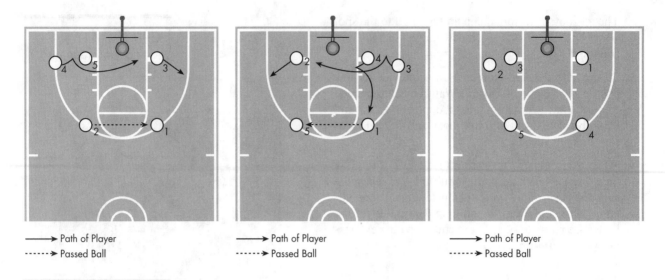

→ Path of Player
----→ Passed Ball

→ Path of Player
----→ Passed Ball

→ Path of Player
----→ Passed Ball

Figure 4.19 (above)
Weak side forward.

3. for a straight drive to the basket

4. to back up and get out of trouble

Once the basic set of the offense has been learned, various entries and special plays can be added to give the offense a different look.

Triple-Post Offense

Although the triple-post offense has been in use for more than 50 years, it is getting renewed respect and attention because of the spectacular success of the NBA's Chicago Bulls during the 1990s and the team's excellent execution of this fine offense. Tex Winter, primary architect of the triple-post offense, has had success using this offense throughout a long and distinguished career at both the collegiate and professional levels.

This offense does not use three post players as the name might suggest. Rather, it utilizes a basic floor-positioning and spacing concept that creates a three-player triangle to initiate the offensive plays. The basic floor positioning is shown in Figure 4.21.

Figure 4.20
Basic offense set.

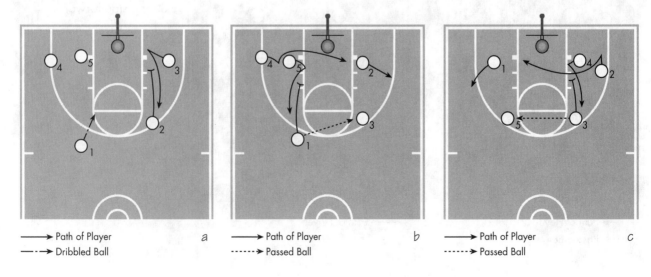

→ Path of Player
--·-→ Dribbled Ball

a

→ Path of Player
----→ Passed Ball

b

→ Path of Player
----→ Passed Ball

c

The floor spacing is essentially a 2-3 offensive set with the center at the lane, where a 45-degree angle is created between the center and the basket. Coach Winter calls this the *line of deployment* (Winter, 1962). Fifteen-foot spacing between the players is essential to this set. The primary function of the offense is to create easier passing lanes to the post player and provide one-on-one situations in front of the basket and between the ball and the basket.

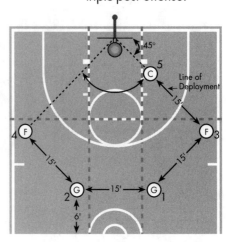

Figure 4.21

Basic floor positioning for triple-post offense.

SKILL 2 | Zone Offense

The zone defenses are designed primarily to concentrate on the offensive player with the ball. They also try to force opponents into taking longer, more difficult shots because of their nature of protecting the lane and basket area. Therefore, zone offenses must find ways to get players open and in as good or close shooting position as possible. The following qualities of successful zone offenses should be considered.

1. Use quick ball movement—fast passing with little dribbling.

2. Don't force shots; be patient and make the defense work.

3. Use ball fakes.

4. Dribble-penetrate gaps in the zone. Hit shot or make a quick pass to an open teammate.

5. Move into seams created by two defensive players and cut toward the basket to force the defense to protect the basket deep in the lane.

6. Pull defense to one side of the floor to cover an overload situation, then use a skip pass over the zone to a teammate on the other side of the court.

7. Look to get the ball inside the lane by hitting the post player, hitting a cutter, or dribble-penetrating.

8. Rebound. Strong offensive rebounding is often the strongest weapon against a zone.

9. The best offense against a zone is to fast break them before the players can get into their set positions.

One theory to attack the zone defense emphasizes using a fast break attack to beat the defense down the floor. Good shots are often available before the defense has time to set up. If the break doesn't produce a shot, the secondary break may.

A second theory is to play an alignment opposite that of the defense. If the defense is using a 1-3-1 zone, use a 2-1-2 or 2-3 alignment on offense. If the zone is a 2-3 or 2-1-2, play a 1-3-1 alignment. The concept here is to overload the zone in the zone's natural gaps or open areas. The defense must move and adjust to prevent good shots. Once the zone adjusts, it is merely playing the same alignment as the offense, which means the offense must continue to pass and move to create new overloads. This constant ball and player movement by the offense causes the defense to continually adjust, which gives the offense an advantage because the defense is reacting and, therefore, moving after the offense. Good shooting opportunities will result.

The following overload offense (Figure 4.22) is simple and can be utilized against either 1-3-1, 2-3, or 2-1-2 zone.

Figure 4.22

Overload zone offense.

⟶ Path of Player

----➤ Passed Ball

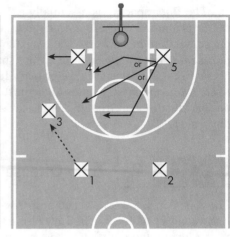

a. Two outside players (X_1 and X_2) are in guard positions 12 to 15 feet apart and above the key. One wing player is on either side of the key and above the free throw line (X_3). Two posts are positioned on both sides of the lane and even with the basket (X_4 and X_5).

b. The ball is passed to the wing from the nearest guard. As the wing receives the pass, the low post on the side nearest the ball moves to the corner. The off-side low post moves to the ball across the lane. The path of the post coming to the ball will vary according to how the defense is playing.

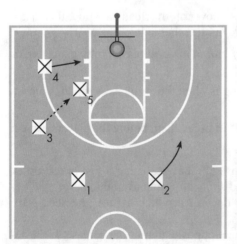

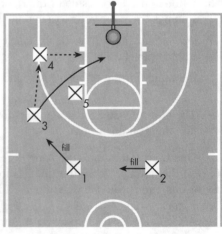

c. The wing looks inside the low post coming to the ball first and makes the pass to him/her, if open. If the post does receive a pass, everyone else should move to an open area for a pass. Post players must attempt to score if the ball is passed inside.

d. If the low post is not open for the pass, the wing passes to the corner and cuts to the basket. If open on the cut, he/she receives a pass from the corner. The guard nearest the vacated wing moves down to fill, and the other positions also are filled.

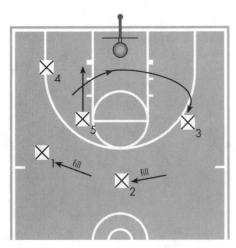

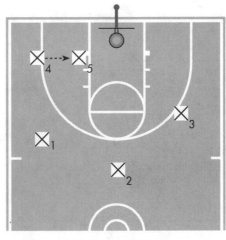

Figure 4.22
Continued.

e. If not open on the cut to the basket, the wing continues through the zone and back to the off-side wing position, and as close to the basket as the defense will allow. As the cutter clears, the post moves down the lane to the baseline, at all times looking for the pass.

f. If open low, the post receives a pass from the corner. If the low post receives a pass, he/she should look for a shot or pass to the off-side wing, which the cutter has filled.

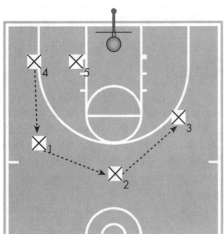

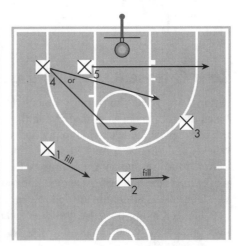

g. If the corner player cannot make the pass to the low post on the baseline, the ball is passed quickly "around the horn" to the off-side wing.

h. As the ball is passed back to the off-side wing, the low post moves to the off-side corner, and the player in the corner throughout the first options now becomes the post and goes to the ball. At this point, the offense has been completed and is ready to begin the same options on the other side of the floor. This is the basic pattern.

Figure 4.22
Continued.

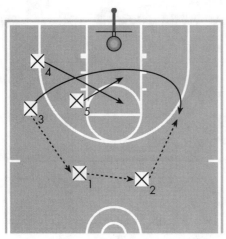
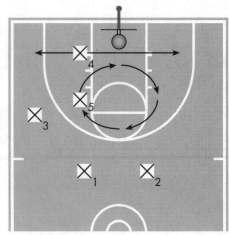

i. If the ball is not passed to the corner, but, rather, back to the point from the wing, the wing still goes through the zone just as if he/she had passed to the corner. The ball is passed back around the off-side and the same shot will be available. The corner player and post player will make the same moves as in the completed pattern.

j. On some occasions it might be desirable for a certain player to play a specific position—the post, for example. If so, a player will be assigned to the position and will remain there. The same pattern is run, and the same objectives remain, except the post and base-line will remain at those positions. This means the player on the baseline has a long distance to cover, but it should be no problem.

Zone Offense (Overload) (Figure 4.22)

Against any zone, the primary objective must be to pass the ball inside the zone. Once the ball has been passed inside the zone, it must collapse to the ball, and then the pass can be made outside for a good shot. To beat a zone, the ball must be passed quickly and the player must go to any open area to receive a pass against a zone. If a player stands in one spot, the zone will adjust to cover that "spot." The longer any player holds the ball against a zone, the more time the zone has to shift and adjust.

One rule is all that is needed to beat any zone: *Pass the ball quickly!*

The following position guidelines can help improve individual play when attacking zone defenses:

POST PLAY (#4 & #5):

1. Give the passer a *target*—get in a *straight line* from the ball → you → basket.
2. Be able to shoot the *hook*—pivot foot parallel to the baseline.
3. Be able to shoot the *power lay-up*—fake, turn, go off both feet.
4. Be able to shoot the *turn-around jumper*—no defensive pressure.
5. *Faking:* Move the ball quickly—show the ball to the defense.
6. Pivot or *drop step* when catching the ball—post-up tough.
7. *Reverse pivot*—shoot, or cross-over dribble and drive.
8. *Set a good pick* across the lane after 3-second count.
9. Receiving defensive pressure or double team—*look to weak-side.*
10. *Rebound*—assume that every shot will miss.

POINT PLAY (#1):

1. Work against one defensive player—don't dribble into a double team.
2. Look at the basket, ball over head, move ball in fakes—throw over the head when possible.
3. Move to open area—step inside.
4. Move the ball—fake, fake, pass.

WING PLAY (#2 & #3):

1. Move around—don't stand in corner; step in and out.
2. Look for crossfire or opposite wing—make v-cuts and always move to rebound.
3. Cut off the outside foot—inside foot points toward point, outside foot to basket or corner.
4. Move the ball—fake, fake, pass.
5. Smallest point or wing player is always responsible for defense.

A third theory of attacking the zone defense is to play the same alignment that the defense uses. If the defense is a 1-3-1 zone, a 1-3-1 offensive alignment is used. If it's a 2-3 zone, a 2-3 alignment is used, and so on. Here, the players are basic working positions and do not change positions except for a quick cut. The ball is moved quickly around the perimeter of the zone until an opportunity presents itself. The purpose of the spot position alignment is to establish one-on-one situations, as the defense is matched up and forced to play what essentially is a sagging man-to-man defense. This can create offensive opportunities such as taking advantage of the placement of special individual talents like size or maneuverability or exploiting weak spots in the sagging defense, which will leave offensive players open.

SKILL 3 Offense Against the Press

Full Court Press Offense Against Zone Presses The initial alignment of the **press offense** is shown in Figure 4.23. The guards break, with the one not getting the ball going to the weak side. The players must stay out of the corners because the most severe defensive pressure can be applied at those points on the court. Player 1 passes the ball inbounds and steps between the pass and the basket for defense. Players 4 and 5 play the middle and sideline—leaving the weak-side open for the guard rotation (3). After the ball comes inbounds, the alignment always should be 2-3.

The following fundamentals should be considered when working against a press:

1. Move to meet most passes (step toward the pass).
2. Keep moving; don't stop. Find openings and move into them.
3. Pass the ball to the middle of the court at every opportunity.
4. Pass the ball across court very little.
5. Upon receiving a pass, turn and look up the court.
6. Pass first, and dribble second.
7. Move the ball up the court.

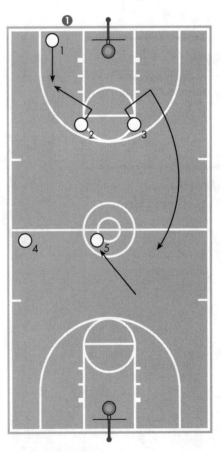

Figure 4.23
Offense against the press.

→ Path of Player

press offense *a type of offense in which positioning can vary from mid-court, to three-quarter, to full court*

8. Be quick, but don't hurry.
9. The player who handles the ball out of bounds or last is responsible for defense until another pass is made.

A team offense against a zone press works best. The first priority is to get the ball inbounds and up court safely. Keep the ball in the middle of the court to counter defensive pressure and to avoid being trapped with the ball. Attack the press when possible by throwing over the press. A few lay-ups or fouls will destroy a press. If a turnover is committed, get back on defense and don't allow the other team to get lay-ups off their press.

Full Court Press Offense Against Man-to-Man All-Out Press Figure 4.24 shows the all-out press alignment to use against a tough man-to-man or all-out press that tries to deny the inbounds pass.

Players 4 and 5 cross and pick for one another, then move to the corners to pick for guards 2 and 3. Guards 2 and 3 can fake-up and sprint long down court or fake-down and go to the ball. Player 1 passes the ball inbounds and moves to the outside of the player he/she passed to. If working against a straight man-to-man, players without the ball should clear-out (go downcourt). Be wary of jump and run presses. In this case, someone must come back to help the teammate with the ball.

Half Court Press Offense When the defense wants to apply a pressure, trapping defense at the half court or mid-court line, a half court press offense should be utilized. A half court press can be attacked in a variety of ways. Figure 4.25 works in most cases.

Figure 4.24 (on left)
All-out press against man-to-man all-out press.

Figure 4.25 (on right)
Half court pass offense.

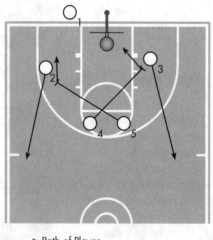

Path of Player

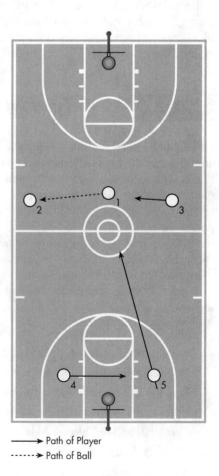

Path of Player
Path of Ball

The ball should be in the middle of the court. Player 1 passes to player 2 (or 3) and splits the defense. Player 3 replaces Player 1 to serve as a safety valve. Player 5 (or 4) breaks to the middle of the court, while 4 replaces 5. Player 2 looks at 1, 5 coming to the middle, or back to 3. The primary objective is to get the ball across the half court line and keep it in the middle of the court when possible.

Any press offense must be able to adjust to the pressure, as the defense will change. Move players and the ball to open area and back to the middle of the court. Avoid passing to the same spot every time. Use short, quick passes and movement to pick the defense apart. All press defenses overplay and will make mistakes, so be ready to take advantage.

SKILL 4 | Fast Break Offense

The fast break is an important part of the transition game and can be a strong component in attacking zone defenses or starting the offense. The Flex or Spots offense discussed earlier also can be used as a fast break or early offense.

When using spots as an early offense, assign players spots numbering according to their talents and strengths (Figure 4.26).

To simplify this offense, the offense can be run on one side only. The offense can be run on either side, but player recognition of situations can be enhanced if it is mastered on one side first. In this case, the offense will run to the right side. This is done to make it appear that the ball is away from the two best shooters. The goal, however, is to flatten out the defense and reverse the ball back to the shooters before the defense can adjust.

Specifically, the ball should be pushed down the court as quickly as possible. If a 2-on-1 or 3-on-2 advantage presents itself, the normal break should be run. If there is no advantage, however, the players should go immediately to their spots, as shown in Figure 4.27.

The offense begins with Player 1 passing the ball to 4 while 5 breaks to the ball to draw the defense toward him/her (Figure 4.28).

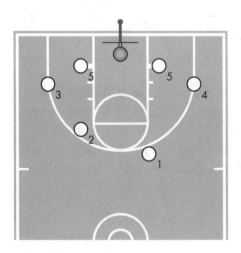

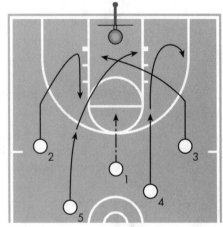

Figure 4.26 (on left)
Assigned player spots for fast break offense.

Figure 4.27 (on right)
Getting to spots in fast break offense.

#1 spot = best ball handler and passer
#2 spot = best outside shooter
#3 spot = second best shooter
#4 spot = strongest rebounding forward
#5 spot = center

⟶ Path of Player
— · —➤ Dribbled Ball

Figure 4.28 (on left)

Beginning of fast break offense.

Figure 4.29 (on right)

Looking for shot in fast break offense.

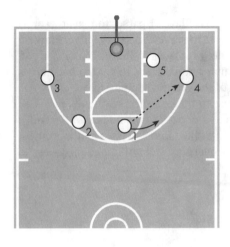

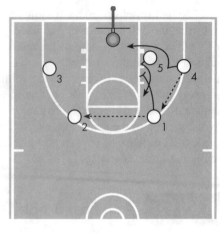

> ──────► Path of Player
> ------► Passed Ball

Figure 4.30

Screen-the-screener play.

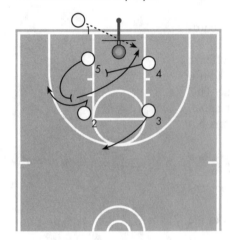

> ──────► Path of Player
> ------► Passed Ball

Figure 4.31

Double screen play.

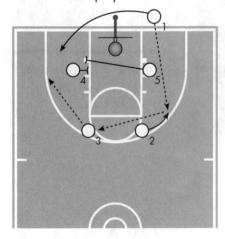

> ──────► Path of Player
> ------► Passed Ball

The ball then is reversed to Player 1, who looks for 2 or 3 for the shot (Figure 4.29). If there is no shot, Player 1 will screen down and begin the basic set offense.

SKILL 5 Out-of-Bounds Plays

The primary objective in all attempts to bring the ball into play from out-of-bounds, from the sidelines or the defensive end line, or even the offensive end line is to get the ball safely inbounds. The following general suggestions should be followed when planning out-of-bounds plays:

1. Keep the plays simple.
2. Take advantage of the best passer, screener, and shooter.
3. The passer must be alert, poised, and deliberate to allow teammates time to set up.
4. Keep opponents guessing at all times. Use similar formations with different plays.
5. Have rebound strength near the basket when the shot is taken.
6. Practice out-of-bounds plays regularly so all players know their assignments.

The following out-of-bounds plays can be used at the *offensive end line*. Each play can be run from either side of the basket. Two plays for each formation will be illustrated.

Box Formation

Screen-the-Screener (Figure 4.30): Player 5 sets screen for 2 as 4 sets the screen for 5. Player 5's defender often is checking Player 2 and lets 5 get lay-up.

In the **double screen** (Figure 4.31): Two low players screen away from Player 1 out of bounds, then two outer players (2 and 3) rotate halfway to reverse the ball. Player 1 steps in behind double screen.

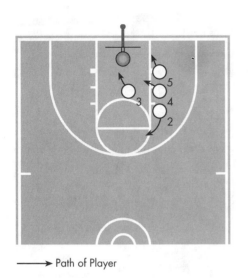

→ Path of Player

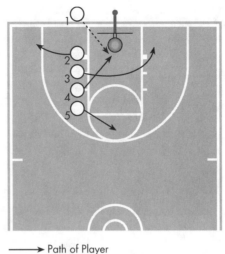

→ Path of Player

- - -→ Passed Ball

Figure 4.32 (on left)
Toss.

Figure 4.33 (on right)
Slant.

Line Formation

Toss (Figure 4.32): Players line up close together and wait until the last moment. The ball is tossed to Player 4 or middle player who uses the board. The rebound is made with Player 2 back.

Slant (Figure 4.33): Players 2, 3, and 5 cut as shown. Player 4 cuts down the middle for a pass from Player 1.

double screen *a screen set by two players*

Foul Line Formation

Cross (Figure 4.34): Player 3 steps forward while 4 and 2 split off 3, with 4 cutting first.

Swing (Figure 4.35): Player 5 breaks outside for pass. Player 2 fakes and then cuts behind double screen set by Players 3 and 4. Player 5 passes to 2 for the shot.

The out-of-bounds plays shown in Figure 4.36 are used to inbound the ball from the sideline.

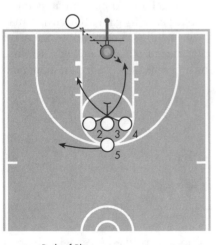

→ Path of Player

- - -→ Passed Ball

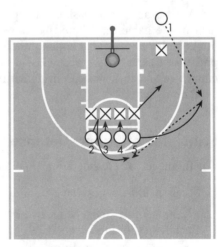

→ Path of Player

- - -→ Passed Ball

Figure 4.34 (on left)
Cross.

Figure 4.35 (on right)
Swing.

Figure 4.36
Sideline out-of-bounds plays.

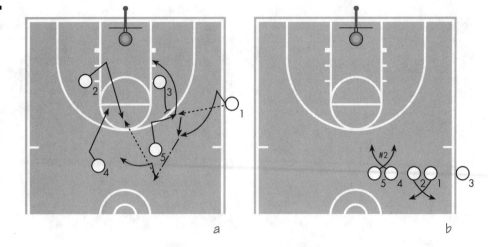

⟶ Path of Player
------➤ Passed Ball
—·—➤ Dribbled Ball

(a) Player 1 passes in to 5, who fakes in and comes toward him/her, 5 returns the pass to 1, who fakes in and then comes around him/her. Player 1 takes a dribble or two and tries to pass to 2 coming up across the foul line. Player 2 looks for 5 cutting off of a screen by 3, or for 4, who makes a quick backdoor cut as Player 2 receives the ball from 1.

(b) From a line formation, players pair up (1 & 2, 4 & 5) and determine which pair will go toward basket and which will go toward mid-court. They cross and move to get open for a pass from 3.

GAME/ACTIVITY STRATEGIES: TEAM DEFENSE

"Team defense can be no stronger than the defensive fundamentals of the individuals playing it" (Wooden, 1966, p. 262).

Coach Wooden's statement highlights how important individual defensive fundamentals are to successful team play. Each individual must do his/her part to contribute to the whole. Team defense, however, does not mean that each individual is solely responsible for offensive outcomes during a game. Teamwork and all-out effort must characterize team defense. Players must be willing to "help their teammates in order to frustrate, stymie, or stop the opposing offense." Outstanding teamwork is required to blend individual skills into a unit that instinctively reacts to every move by the opponents.

Most coaches and basketball experts consider defense to be the one component of the game that should be consistent from game to game. Offensive play might suffer from cold shooting, a bad night, or inability to respond to defensive pressure. Despite those obstacles, a team can stay in a game or keep it close enough to snatch victory from defeat if its own defense is causing the opponent similar problems.

Principles of Sound Defense

The following are considerations to mold an effective defense:

1. Team members must have a *desire* to play defense.

2. Team members must be individually sound and well-schooled in the defensive techniques, or fundamentals.

3. The team attitude should be that a team effort keeps the player with the ball from scoring; players will help teammates when necessary.

4. Team effort requires *communication.* Players must *talk* or use their voices to let others know where they are, what is happening behind them, and alert each other about trouble situations.

5. Definite responsibilities should be established to counter offensive maneuvers and for rebounding.

6. The defensive player guarding the offensive player with the ball should challenge him/her.

7. Players must recognize the need to guard the weak-side player in movements toward the ball.

8. Defensive players should make the opponent work to get the ball.

9. Team defense should work to prevent the ball from moving into scoring areas (see Figure 4.37). Area X is a critical scoring area. Area Y must be defended against the 3-point shot. Area Z is defended in a half court press.

10. Players must automatically know how to play the pick and roll, the split-the-post play, and the pass and go.

Figure 4.37

Preventing ball from moving into scoring areas.

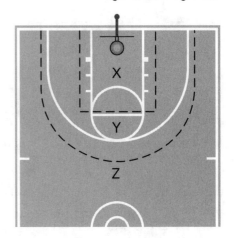

Types of Defenses

Three general types of defense are characteristic of today's game of basketball: the man-to-man, the zone, and the press. The basic principle for the man-to-man defense is to assign each player to an individual opponent and the player's primary responsibility is to stop the offensive player from scoring. The zone defense differs in that the defender is assigned a specific area of the court to cover and the major responsibility is to prevent *any* opponent from scoring in his/her area. The press defense may be either in a man-to-man form or in a zone. The goal of a press is to put constant pressure on the opponents. This pressure can be applied over the entire length of the court, from three-fourths court, or from half court.

SKILL 6 | Man-to-Man Defense

In a **man-to-man** defense, each player must help his/her teammates whenever possible. This requires good defensive positioning—the most important aspect of team defense. Team defense begins when a team loses possession of the ball. All players should sprint back toward the area in which the player they are assigned to usually plays. Adjusting from offense to defense quickly is critical to successful team defense.

The amount of pressure a team wants to apply in its defense will help determine at what point on the court each member of the defense will pick up his/her man. Man-to-man pressure can be applied at any point on the court. Usually, teams will pick-up their man at half court or "sag" back toward the defensive lane area.

In playing man-to-man half court team defense, the court can be divided into two halves (see Figure 4.38). The half of the court where the ball is positioned is called the *strong side* or *ball side.* The half of the court that is away from the ball is known as the *weak side* or *help side* of the court.

Typically, players on the help side of the court sag toward the ball side or move away from their assigned opponent to be able to help a teammate if necessary. Players on the ball side apply pressure to the ball and try to deny passes on this side of the floor. The following defensive rules for each player in a man-to-man defense can be applied to this "helping" team defense.

man-to-man *a team defense in which each defensive player is assigned to guard a specific opponent*

Figure 4.38

Man-to-man half court team defense.

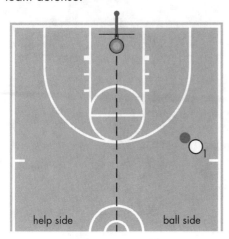

help side   ball side

1. *Outside player guarding the ball*

   a. Don't let the opponent handle the ball comfortably. Apply pressure.

   b. Square up, force the ball to the inside or toward the help side of the court.

2. *Outside player away from the ball* (help side)

   a. Discourage a high-post pass or inside dribble.

   b. Go with the player and don't position yourself above ball level.

3. *Inside player on ball side*

   a. Don't let player catch the ball inside the free throw line extended.

   b. Cover a low post three-fourths of body in front, a medium post one-half body in front, and behind a high-post toward the ball side. Remember to reverse pivot to rebound.

4. *Inside player away from ball* (help side)

   a. Don't let the offensive player come inside or across the lane to catch a ball.

   b. Be ready to help or support the defensive post player.

Figures 4.39 and 4.40 show the defensive positioning when the ball is at the guard position and at the forward position, respectively. *Defensive positions with the ball at the guard position:* X_1, X_4, and X_5 are on the ball side and play their opponents aggressively. Players X_2 and X_3 are on the help side and sag toward the ball side of the court. *Defensive positions with the ball at the forward position:* Players X_1, X_4, and X_5 are still on the ball side and play their opponents aggressively. Notice that X_1 and X_5 have moved toward the ball. X_2 and X_3 are still on the help side but move farther away from their opponents toward the ball.

It is important that all defensive players remember to keep their eyes on the ball and on their opponent. To do this properly, the defensive player must position himself/herself between the ball and offensive opponent he/she is assigned to defend. This is known as the **ball-your-opponent** principle. The ball-your-opponent positioning for guards and forwards is shown in Figures 4.41 and 4.42, respectively.

ball your opponent *a defensive principle in which the player positions himself/herself between the ball and the offensive opponents*

Figure 4.39 (on left)

Man-to-man defensive positioning at guard position.

Figure 4.40 (on right)

Man-to-man defensive positioning at forward position.

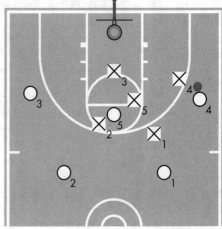

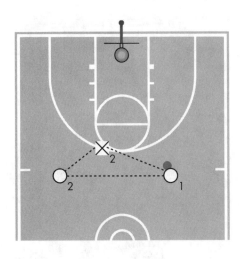

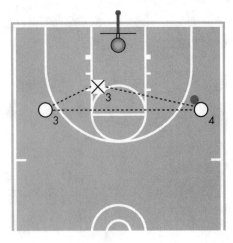

Figure 4.41 (on left)
Ball-your-opponent position for guards.

Figure 4.42 (on right)
Ball-your-opponent position for forwards (wings).

Defending the Screen

Offenses use many screens during the course of a game in trying to free one of their players for an open shot or path to the basket. Therefore, the defense has to know how it is going to execute defending the screens. Two main philosophies apply to defending the screen.

1. Have defenders switch players to defend.
2. Slide through the screen and continue guarding the same offensive player.

Sliding through the screen is accepted as the standard defensive philosophy. The following guidelines should be noted for the various circumstances that occur when screens are set during a game.

1. When a teammate's player has the ball and your player *goes behind* the offensive player with the ball, *you should go between* the player with the ball and your teammate.
2. When your teammate's player has the ball and your player *goes between* the player with the ball and your teammate, *you should go behind* your teammate.
3. The defensive player guarding the ball has a preference as far as position is concerned. Communication between the defensive players is important in successfully defending the screen. When the player sliding through is going between the ball and a teammate, a step back by the teammate will help. When the player sliding through is going behind the screen, his/her teammate should tighten up on the defense.
4. The player defending the screener also can help his/her teammate by stepping out into the path of the ball handler. This will allow the defensive teammate on the ball enough time to slide through. This is the point, however, at which the offense may execute the *pick and roll.* The defender who steps out must be prepared to move quickly back into position to stop the screener from opening up to the basket. Also, weak-side help must be coming to support the defense.

Figures 4.43 and 4.44 illustrate the **step-out** and **slide-through** techniques, respectively. *Step-out technique:* As Player O4 sets a screen on X1, X4 steps out in O1's path as if to switch. X1 fights over the top of the screen. When O4 cuts for basket, X4 goes also, attempting to stay between O4 and the ball.

Slide-through technique: On the left, Player O1 passes to O2 and sets a screen. As O2 dribbles off screen, defensive player X2 slides through and remains with O2. On the right, Player O3 uses dribbling screen for O4. As O4 comes outside O3, X3 steps back to allow X4 to slide through and remain with O4.

step-out *a defensive technique in which the player defending the screener helps teammates by moving out into the path of the ball handler*
slide-through *a defensive technique in which the defensive player glides through the screen and continues guarding the same offensive player*

Figure 4.43 (on left)
Step-out technique.

Figure 4.44 (on right)
Slide-through technique.

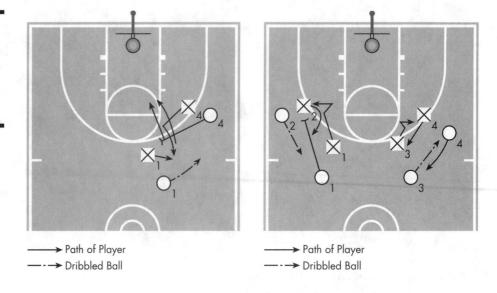

———▶ Path of Player
— · —▶ Dribbled Ball

———▶ Path of Player
— · —▶ Dribbled Ball

Switching

switching picking up any offensive player other than the one the defensive player is normally guarding

Switching may be the best defensive reaction to a screen play under some circumstances. The following hints apply to switching on defense.

1. Don't switch unless you have to.
2. The back player always calls the switch, as he/she is in the best position to make the quick change and to decide whether a switch is necessary (see Figure 4.45).

Figure 4.45
Switching.

The back player, Player 1, in the white jersey, calls the switch. He then covers the ball handler and lets his teammate cover the screener, who was Player 1's former opponent.

3. Keep talking, and let a teammate with his/her back to the screen know that the screen is there by yelling, "Pick, watch the pick."
4. If a switch is called, react fast and pick up the player who screens you, while your teammate takes your previous offensive opponent.

Trapping

Trapping the player with the ball to steal the ball or force a turnover requires team coordination. Some variations of man-to-man defense use trapping techniques to try to rattle the opposing teams. Trapping tactics tend to work best if the following situations present themselves:

1. When the offense is near a sideline; the sideline acts as another defender.
2. When offensive guards cross or when the offensive guard with the ball turns his/her back away from the second defensive guard.
3. When the offensive post receives a pass.

When a guard sets a trap (double-team), the wing or forward opposite the ball comes out to cover the free offensive guard and the wing or forward on the side of the ball immediately plays in front of his/her man. The center usually protects the basket by applying zone principles. The two players most likely to receive an offensive pass from the trap are the guard without the ball and the forward on the ball side. A pass to either one of these players must be denied. Trapping is an aggressive defensive maneuver, and fouling often occurs because of the defender's aggressiveness. This has to be watched so the defense doesn't allow the offense to escape the pressure and perhaps score points from the resulting foul shots.

trapping (double-teaming) *a defensive maneuver in which two defenders confine an offensive player with the ball and attempt to prevent successful completion of a pass*

Man-to-Man Team Defense Drills

The following team defensive drills will help players to learn appropriate habits for good defensive play in given situations. It is best to start with two-against-two drills, followed by three-on-three, four-on-four, and finally adding the fifth player to develop the full team defense.

Drill #71: Two-against-Two at Guard Positions

In the Two-against-Two at Guard Position drill, Players O_1 and O_2 make a cross maneuver in Area C outside the shooting range or effective scoring range; defensive players X_1 and X_2 slide through and stay with their assigned opponents. When O_1 dribbles as shown in Figure 4.46, X_1 goes with him/her. Player O_2, cutting over the top of O_1 to receive the ball and take away on a dribble, is outside the effective shooting range, so X_2 will slide through behind O_1, and go between X_1 and O_1. While doing this, X_1 may have to drop off slightly to allow X_2 to slide through.

Here the use of the voice begins, and X_1 and X_2 communicate constantly, talking so that each knows what the other is going to do. Player X_1 could say, "Slide through, slide through, stay with him/her," etc. Player X_2's response might be, "I have him/[her], I have him/[her]." Player X_1 could even aid X_2 by placing his/her hands on X_2's hips and guiding him/her through.

Figure 4.46
Two-against-two.

⟶ Path of Player
┄┄► Passed Ball
—·—► Dribbled Ball

Figure 4.47
Guard-forward maneuver
drill.

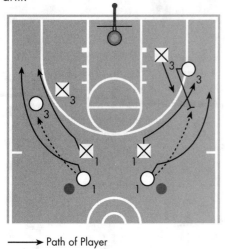

Figure 4.47
Guard-forward maneuver
drill.

——▶ Path of Player
------▶ Passed Ball

Drill #72: Guard-Forward Maneuver Drill

Go to a Guard-Forward Maneuver drill. Teach the proper defensive mechanics for those areas. Figure 4.47 gives a common guard-forward maneuver with Player 1 passing to 3 and cutting to the outside for an outside screen. If 3 is outside the effective shooting range for 1, then X_3 should loosen up slightly and call for X_1 to slide through. Player X_1 will slide through between 3 and X_3 and stay with 1. Players X_1 and X_3 must maintain constant voice communication.

Drill #73: Zoning Area A Drill

Before a team defense can be effective, it must be able to prevent passes into area X—the "dangerous zone" or vital scoring area. All players should be schooled in the Zoning Area X Drill (Figure 4.48). Players 1, 2, 3, and 4 pass the ball around rapidly in an effort to work the ball into Area X to Player 5. Player 5 works and maneuvers to get open, but X_5 defenses him/her by checking, fronting, siding, stepping in front of him/her to block his/her moves—doing anything to prevent the pass inside to 5—anything that is within the rules. Player X_5 must make every effort to stay between 5 and the ball to prevent a pass inside to the vital scoring area.

Drill #74: Three-Against-Three Drill

After teaching two-against-two defensive maneuvers, go to three-against-three, using the guard, forward, and pivot-post positions on defense. Now the defensive maneuvers that must be used when the ball goes into the pivot-post position must be taught. If offensive players cut by the pivot-post player in screening maneuvers, the over-the-top principle of sticking tight must apply and be practiced. If screens are effective, the "help" situation must be applied—with voice communication used to the fullest extent to be sure that assignments are straight, and that pressure is applied to the player with the ball. In the Three-Against-Three Drill (Figure 4.49), when Player O_1 passes in to O_3, he/she may take any of the movement options indicated, and scrimmage play progresses from there to an actual game situation. When either Player O_1 or O_3 passes in to O_5 at the pivot-post position, if he/she takes the option of breaking past O_5 to secure a screen, the proper defense is to be worked out so defensive team assignments are clearly defined.

Figure 4.48 (on left)
Zoning area X drill.

Figure 4.49 (on right)
Three-against-three drill.

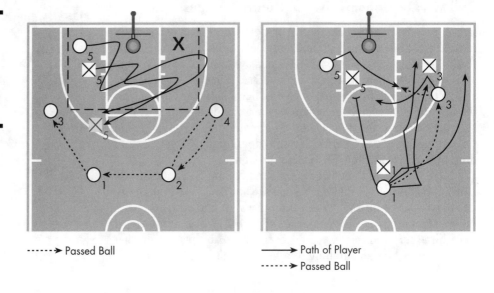

------▶ Passed Ball

——▶ Path of Player
------▶ Passed Ball

Drill #75: Four-Against-Four Drill

The Four-Against-Four Drill (Figure 4.50) promotes further development in mastering the team defense. It throws in the guard maneuvers and the proper defending moves, the guard-forward moves, with proper defending, defending the pivot-post area (preventing passes thereto), and defending moves made over and around the pivot-post, once the ball is passed in to that position.

Drill #76: Five-Against-Five Drill

Now the team should be ready to practice the Five-Against-Five Drill (Figure 4.51), with the defensive team movements being coordinated against the many complicated offensive moves. The defense is coordinated as a team, making sure all players know their assignments and what they must do to handle each situation.

Drill #77: Learning to Play the Triangle

In Learning to Play the Triangle (Figure 4.52), the offensive players move the ball around rapidly from player to player. The defensive players work on properly defending the player with the ball (X_1); on defending properly to make the player on the ball-side of the floor work hard to get the ball (X_3) (note foot position of X_3); on defending the weak-side player and not letting that player break toward the ball, ahead of the defensive player, to receive the ball in the scoring area (X_4).

Note the dotted lines giving the two imaginary lines that the defensive players must be aware of and play at all times—the line from the opponent to the ball, and the line from the opponent to the basket. When the opponent does not have the ball, the defensive player must make adjustments in position between these two lines based on the speed of the opponent, distance from the ball, position of the ball, his/her own speed, speed of opponent's passing, and the defensive application being made at the time. When the opponent has the ball, only one line application is to be made—the imaginary line from the opponent to the basket—and because his/her opponent has the ball, this defensive player must apply pressure.

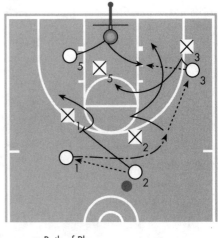

Figure 4.50
Four-against-four drill.

→ Path of Player
----→ Passed Ball
—·→ Dribbled Ball

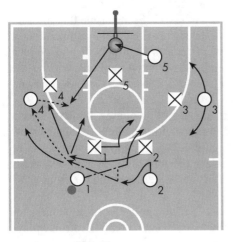

→ Path of Player
----→ Passed Ball
—·→ Dribbled Ball

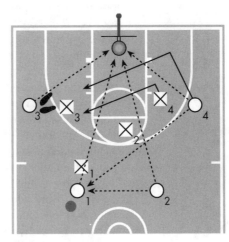

→ Path of Player
----→ Passed Ball

Figure 4.51 (on left)
Five-against-five drill.

Figure 4.52 (on right)
Playing the triangle.

SKILL 7 | Zone Defenses

zone *a team defense in which each player is responsible for an assigned area of the court rather than a specific opponent*

Zone defenses are designed to allow the defensive team to protect the area close to the basket. The idea is to make short shots difficult to obtain and give the defense better rebound positioning and, perhaps, more opportunity to begin the transition from defense to offense via the fast break. The following zone defense principles should be remembered.

1. Concentrate on position, stance, and good sound defensive maneuvers.
2. Focus attention on the ball, and shift rapidly with each movement of the ball.
3. Attack the player with the ball when in your defensive zone.
4. When no player is in your zone coverage area, find the area that has more than one player in it, and move in to help on the extra coverage.
5. When more than one player is in your zone, and none has the ball, cover the player nearest the ball.
6. Don't allow a player with the ball to drive around you.
7. When an offensive player cuts through the zone near the ball, guard him/her man-for-man until no longer in position to receive the pass.
8. Do not allow the ball to penetrate to the post or baseline with one pass.
9. Keep the hands up and feet moving at all times. Cut off the passing lanes by moving the hands.
10. Put defensive pressure on every shot taken.
11. After a shot, block out the offensive player in your area, then go for the ball.
12. Hustle and communicate in a zone defense. Constantly talk about the movement of the offensive players.
13. Do your own job *and* help out teammates.

Figure 4.53 (on top)
2-3 zone defense with coverage responsibilities.

Figure 4.54 (on bottom)
Weak areas in 2-3 zone.

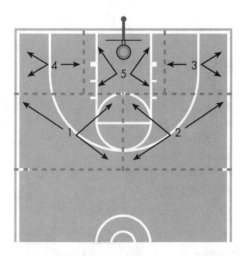

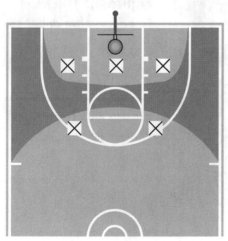

Types of Zone Defense

Among the most common or orthodox of the many zone defenses are the: 1-3-1, 1-2-2, 2-3, 3-2, and 2-1-2. Some argue that the 1-2-2 and the 3-2 zones are really the same as the 2-1-2 and 2-3 zones. Because of the 3-point shot in today's high school and college games, the 2-3 zone is the most frequently used and will be the focus of this discussion. Figure 4.53 illustrates the 2-3 zone and player coverage area responsibilities.

This defense is strong in the lane of pivot area. It also is strong in the corners and baseline. It allows for excellent rebound coverage. The shaded areas in Figure 4.54 highlight the weak spots of the 2-3 zone. The 2-3 is weak in the foul line and high-post areas and weak between the two lines of the defense, and the front areas can be easily overloaded.

The 2-3 zone and the 2-1-2 zone apply the same zoning responsibilities or shifts by the teams. Figure 4.55 illustrates players' positions at various ball locations for either the 2-3 or the 2-1-2 zone.

a   Ball at Point

b   Ball at Wing

Figure 4.55

Player positions at various ball locations for 2-3 or 2-1-2 zone.

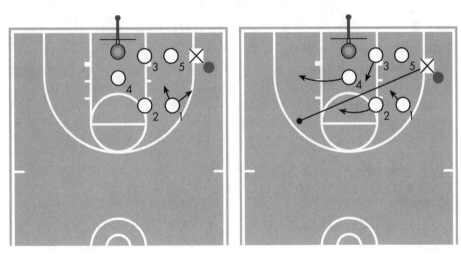

c   Ball in Corner

d   Skip Pass from Corner

(a) Players 1 and 2 cover the free throw line area to stop the high post pass, but move with the ball to cover the wing. If the ball goes to a wing (b), 1 takes the ball and 2 goes to the high-post area. If the ball goes to the corner (c), the ball side wing (1) drops to front any low post while 2 takes the high-post and lane area. When the ball is at the point (d), one of the guards (either 1 or 2) must take the ball, rotating to the strong side.

Player 3 takes the middle area (a–d), making any high-post shoot over him/her. Player 3 tries to stay between the ball and the basket. Also, 3 must block off the pivot and go for every rebound.

Players 4 and 5 cover the baseline area (a–d). They must go to the corner to cover the ball and play the offensive player as if in a man-to-man defense. They cannot allow anyone to drive the baseline. The player on the weak-side must move around, get all weak-side rebounds, and prepare to help cover the wing and corner if a skip pass is thrown to the area.

Strengths and weaknesses of the 2-1-2, 1-2-2, 1-3-1, and the 3-2 zones are highlighted and illustrated in Figures 4.56–4.59.

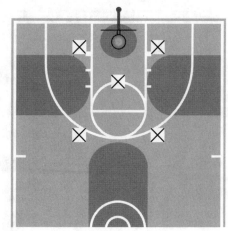

2-1-2 Zone (Figure 4.56)

STRENGTHS:

1. Strong in pivot and corners
2. Strong at foul-line area
3. Good rebound coverage
4. Excellent position to start fast break attack

WEAKNESSES:

1. Vulnerable at good jump shot areas (free throw line extended)
2. Gives up good shots at top of circle

1-2-2 Zone (Figure 4.57)

STRENGTHS:

1. Strong against outside shooting teams
2. Provides excellent fast break opportunities

WEAKNESSES:

1. Weak in the corners
2. Weak against strong post player in pivot area

Figure 4.58
1-3-1 zone.

1-3-1 Zone (Figure 4.58)

STRENGTHS:

1. Strong in foul line area
2. Helps combat overload offenses
3. Good coverage in jump shot areas

WEAKNESSES:

1. Vulnerable to good corner shooters
2. Rebounding areas not well covered
3. Vulnerable along baseline for short jump shots

3-2 Zone (Figure 4.59)

STRENGTHS:

1. Good against outside shooting teams
2. Excellent to start fast break attack
3. Takes away the drive from the middle

WEAKNESSES:

1. Weak in the corners
2. Vulnerable in the middle or foul line area
3. Can be overlooked easily

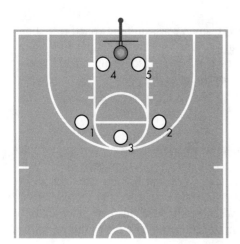 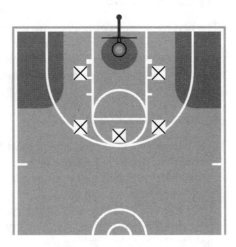

Figure 4.59
3-2 zone.

SKILL 8 | Pressing Defense

press a team defense that may be either man-to-man or zone at any point on the floor

pressing defense a forcing type of defense in which the offense is picked up farther away from the basket than normal; press may be half-court, three-quarter court, or full court

turnover any loss of ball possession caused by a violation

Full-court and half-court **presses** are **pressing defenses** developed primarily to put pressure on the offensive team with the hope of producing errors in judgment and a **turnover** by the offense. The net result of such mistakes is usually an easy basket for the pressing team, and at worst, possession of the ball.

Strategically, a pressing defense can be used for several reasons:

1. *To dictate the tempo of the game.* A pressing defense is used to speed up the tempo of the game and not allow the other team to set the pace of the game.

2. *To disrupt the offense of a poor-ball-handling or inexperienced team.* Bad passes and the inability by the offense to play its style is often the result of a good press.

3. *To place a premium on conditioning.* A team that is well-conditioned and can play at an intense level, both mentally and physically throughout the game, has a huge advantage, especially late into the game when the opponent begins to tire and becomes frustrated by the constant pressure.

4. *To "energize" a team that is behind or not playing well.* Often, a pressing defense can get the players out of the doldrums of a poor performance and create the energy to get back into the game when the team has fallen behind.

5. *To place a premium on teamwork and cooperation.* To play a full-court press properly, a team must have the complete cooperation of all five players in helping out, talking to each other, and switching when necessary. Cooperative defensive play often translates into cooperative offensive play as well. The press is an excellent way to stimulate hustle and team spirit.

6. *To facilitate the fast break.* The possibility of intercepting passes—which often results in quick, easy baskets—puts added pressure on the opponent.

Not every team is equipped to play a pressing defense. All five players have to be able to cover the court quickly and anticipate the offense's next action. It is not necessarily a good idea to press another team if the players on the pressing team are not able to truly apply pressure on the offense. A pressing team should play the offense tight at all times all over the court. The players must talk to one another constantly and try not to foul unnecessarily, which would allow the offense to escape the pressure. Hard work and effort are the cornerstones to a pressing defense.

Types of Presses

The two basic types of presses are the man-to-man press and the zone press. Each type can be used at any point on the court at any time in the game. *Full court, three-quarter court,* and *half-court* presses can be utilized, using either type of press, to harass and disrupt the offensive movement of the ball.

Man-to-Man Press

man-to-man press similar to the man-to-man defense, in which each defensive player puts pressure on an assigned opponent

double team a defensive tactic of using two players to guard the player who has the ball

Like the man-to-man defense, the **man-to-man press** uses the concept of each defensive player putting pressure on an assigned opponent. Though each player is responsible to pressure an opposing player, teamwork and helping are vital to the success of a man-to-man press. A press is a gambling defense, and each defensive player must be ready to help a teammate when he/she loses his/her opponent or to apply **double-team** pressure at the appropriate moment. The following principles apply to the man-to-man press:

1. When pressuring the ball, don't allow the opponent to drive by you.

2. Try to force the ball to the outside. This will allow you to utilize the sideline like an extra defensive player. Also, forcing the ball from the middle of the court takes away passing lanes from the offense.

3. If the ball-handler uses up his/her dribble, apply even more pressure to prevent him/her from using easy-vision or easy-passing lanes.

4. Try to force a **lob pass** or bounce pass. These passes are slower and easier to steal and anticipate.

   lob pass a pass with a high arc

5. If the ball handler turns his/her back to the inside when near a sideline or the mid-court line, "jump" or double-team the ball with the nearest defensive teammate. To be effective, the defense must anticipate and quickly apply this type of pressure.

6. If a teammate loses coverage on his/her opponent, quickly go to the basket area to prevent easy baskets by the offense.

7. Anticipate where the next pass may go, and tighten up on potential receivers.

Zone Presses

Again, the **zone press** is similar to any zone half-court defense. The defensive players are assigned to cover an area of the court and *anyone* in that area rather than an assigned opponent. The five basic zone press variations are the 1-2-1-1, the 2-2-1, the 1-2-2, the 1-3-1, and the 2-1-2. Principles of these zone variations are the following:

zone press similar to zone defense, in which defensive players are assigned to cover an area of the court and anyone in that area

1. Play the ball rather than an opponent.

2. Try to force lob passes, which are slower and easier to intercept.

3. Force the ball away from the middle toward the sidelines. The best places to trap or double-team an opponent are near the sidelines or the corners of the court.

4. When not guarding the ball, other defenders become potential interceptors or double-teamers. Be ready to anticipate the ball handler's next move and watch the ball for opportunities to wreck the offense's plans.

5. If the offense completes a pass over the defense, retreat quickly to regroup and play aggressively. Don't concede anything to the offense.

6. Force the opponent to hurry, which will result in bad decisions and mistakes on which the defense can capitalize.

Press Drills

The following press drill can be used to teach the basic principles of the zone press.

Drill #78: Press Drill

The Press Drill (Figure 4.60) starts out with a two-on-one situation (a). After the offense scores, or the defense gets a rebound, the defensive player (X₁) will immediately step out of bounds and throw an inbounds pass to either X₂ or X₃, who enters the floor below the free throw line extended (b).

As soon as the defensive player (X₁) steps out of bounds for the inbounds pass, the two offensive players O₁ and O₂ take up defensive positions around the free throw line, and O₃ and O₄ will enter from half-court (b). The three X players work

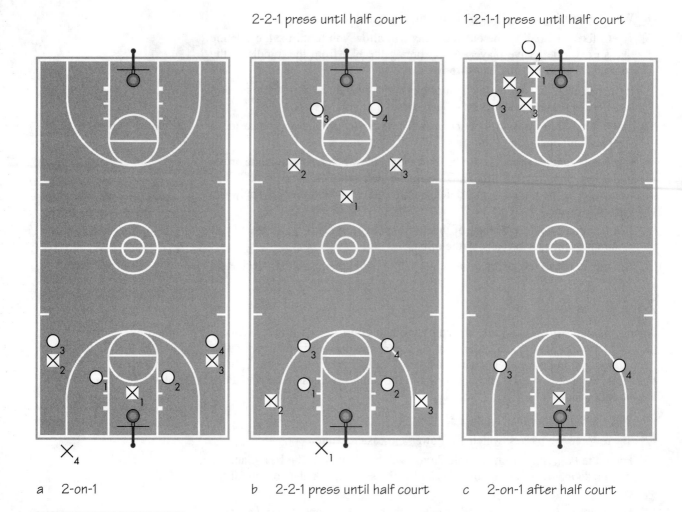

a 2-on-1   b   2-2-1 press until half court   c   2-on-1 after half court

Figure 4.60

Press drill.

the ball up court against the four O players. As the ball crosses half court, O_1 and O_2 drop out.

Figure 4.60 (b) shows the 2-2-1 press with four defensive and three offensive players. The three-on-two play develops after the ball crosses half court. As soon as the offense scores or the defense rebounds, a defensive player O_4 steps out of bounds, passing inbound to O_3. X_1, X_2, and X_3 now become defensive players denying any inbound passes.

Figure 4.60 (c) shows the 1-2 press with two offensive players O_3 and O_4 bringing the ball up court against X_1, X_2, and X_3. The double teams continue until the ball crosses half court, then the three defensive players drop off. At that time, X_4 steps on the court with O_3 and O_4 trying to score. This sets up the drill to start over again.

The X and O players rotate clockwise each time prior to the two-on-one situation, which restarts the drill. The drill probably will end after players have rotated back to their starting positions. The defense will try to score after any steal or turnover, and the drill resumes at that point.

Note: The most fundamental rule of the pressing defense is: *Never allow the ball to go into the middle of the court either by pass or by dribble.* Three-quarter court presses and half-court presses use similar tactics to trap and force the offense without as much gambling and chance of error. Again, the formations can be the same as discussed earlier. In the half-court set, the 1-3-1 press can be quite effective.

Anticipating an opponent's strategy is a function of preparation. Teams must prepare diligently to perfect their own style of play, support their philosophies, and develop their skills to become a team that others consider formidable. Often just as important is a team's preparation for the next opponent. Many coaches/teachers believe as I do that preparing a team to execute its own offense, defense, transitions, inbound plays, and other game situations is of fundamental and of first-priority importance. Worrying about an opponent is not going to make a team better. Teams must be good at what they do before showing much concern for an opponent.

"Games are won on the practice floor" is an old but important cliché. Teams that are prepared give themselves an excellent chance to be successful. Thus, as a team concentrates on its preparation for playing its game, attention should be given to opponents' tendencies. Four mechanisms that can be utilized to better know an opponent's tendencies and then be able to use this knowledge during competition are scouting, game preparation, time-outs, and substitutions.

ANTICIPATING OPPONENTS' STRATEGIES

Scouting

Scouting allows a team to develop and acquire knowledge about an opponent. The aim of scouting is to determine what effect an opponent's strategy or tendencies will have on the team. Using scouting information in this way allows a team to prepare for an opponent in practice while developing its game plan. It also gives the team the opportunity to prepare its substitution patterns for the upcoming game.

scouting obtaining information about an opponent before playing a game

In developing a scouting report on an opponent, a scout can analyze and look for a number of factors. It is probably best to limit the information and look for the most important factors—team offense, team defense, team tendencies, and individual characteristics of the opposing players. The following questions should be considered for each of these factors:

TEAM OFFENSE

1. What type of half-court offense does the opponent prefer?
2. What is the strength of the half-court offense?
3. What are the offensive tendencies? Does the opponent utilize screens? Look to certain players to score? Have favorite plays? Attempt variations of the half court offense?
4. Is this a fast-breaking team?
5. When does the team fast break and does it have a secondary break?
6. Who are the key rebounders?

TEAM DEFENSE

1. What is the basic defense the opponent utilizes? Zone or man-to-man?
2. What type of zone, and how is it played?
3. In a man-to-man, does the team try to deny passes? When does the team play tight? Does the team sag? Switch? How does the team play the post? How does it play the 3-point shot?
4. Does the opponent press and, if so, what type of press and what is it trying to accomplish?

TEAM TENDENCIES

1. Does the opponent run its offense to the same side each time or does it vary the initial attack?

2. Can the guards take pressure?

3. Does the team prefer the jump shot, or like to drive?

4. Does the opponent have favorite out-of-bounds plays?

5. What is the substitution pattern?

INDIVIDUAL CHARACTERISTICS

1. For each player, what is his/her name, number, height, weight, position, speed, condition, temperament, handedness, jumping ability, shooting ability, defensive ability, type of shots preferred, and habits (for example, always dribbles before shooting).

2. Can he/she be faked? Pressed?

3. Is he/she a driver or a perimeter shooter?

4. What does the post player prefer to do?

Game Preparation (Game Plan)

Game preparation includes mental and physical work. Mentally, a team must believe in its game plan and its abilities. The team must know the opponent's style of offense and defense (taken from the scouting report). Each player must know both the opponent's strengths and weaknesses. Players must learn the individual match-ups and individual tendencies.

Physically, preparation deals with how the team plans to play its style versus the opponent. This means that the fundamentals of offense, defense, transitions, pressing, press offense, out-of-bounds plays, and special plays are practiced for perfection. Last, conditioning may be the best way to anticipate an opponent's strategy because a team's hustle, effort, and condition will counter or equalize most opponents' strategies.

A final note on preparing a game plan should be stressed: The plan should be as simple as possible. All too often a team gets carried away with scouting reports and game plans and tries to do more than it's capable of. The end result may be a disaster. A team often out-foxes itself by trying to be too clever. The best strategy to counter opponents' strategies is to out-play, to out-execute, and to out-hustle the opponent.

Time-outs

time-out a designated period of time a coach or players can take to make changes in game strategy, derail opponents, correct mistakes, and prepare players

Depending on the level of play, each team has several **time-outs** in which to attempt to derail an opponent. In college basketball, each team has four full-time time-outs and two 20-second time-outs per game. The time-out is an excellent tool to help anticipate or counter an opponent's strategy.

The following reasons justify use of a time-out:

1. *To make changes in game strategy.* If the opponent has taken you by surprise, a time-out gives a team a chance to get organized and determine future strategies. If a weakness is spotted in the opponent, a time-out is useful in organizing an attack.

2. *To stop a rally by an opponent.* When the opponent is in "the zone" and "hot," a time-out to make defensive adjustments is usually wise.

3. *To correct mistakes or give instruction.* If players are forgetting fundamentals or developing tendencies that the opponent is taking advantage of, a time-out will remind, instruct, and inform players.

4. *To prepare players for the final moments of a tight game.* A time-out at the end of a game can be utilized to set up the last shot or to determine the defense and strategy to use to defend against the last shot. This is also the time to prepare the team for a series of possible events for both offense and defense. Strategies include whom to foul to stop the clock, when this would be appropriate, and what to do if a free throw is made or missed. When protecting a lead, a time-out toward the end of the game allows the team to know who will handle the ball and whether to "run the clock" or try to score more points. Appropriate use of the time-out is often the difference between anticipating the opponent's next move and overcoming a strategy to win the game or failing to stop the opponent and losing.

Substitutions

Using **substitutions** to anticipate the opponent's game plan or to control the tempo of the game is an extremely important strategy. Substitutions can be made to match up or to counter the substitutions of an opponent. Often at the end of a game, a better defensive player may enter the game to help stop the opponent. A player with special offensive skills (a 3-point shooter, a good driver, a foul shooter) can be substituted to take advantage of his/her strengths matched to the team's needs. Also, if the occasion dictates, the best offensive, defensive, rebounding, ball control, or pressing team can be substituted to improve the team's chances of meeting its current needs. If an individual opponent is hurting the team, a defensive substitution may be necessary, or if one of the players is "off," a change may help overall team play. Substitutions are useful in countering an opponent's moves and can help adjust to the characteristics of the opponent.

substitutions players who enter the game to match up or counter opponents

ADJUSTING TO CHARACTERISTICS OF OPPONENTS

Basketball is a game of match-ups. Each team is trying to gain an advantage or neutralize an opponent's advantage by establishing the best match-ups possible based on the players' characteristics. Generally speaking, teams want to match speed with speed, height with height, and weight with weight, but it is not always possible for teams to match up personnel based on the same physical characteristics. Therefore, teams should focus on match-ups that can give an advantage to the team and be aware of match-ups that could hurt the team.

With regard to height and size, if the opponent has a bigger, taller, heavier player that can't be matched, these ideas should be considered:

1. When rebounding, precise blocking out by the smaller player can neutralize the taller opponent. Elbows and arms should be wide and firm to help hold the established position.

2. If the taller opponent has position on the boards, try to out-maneuver him/her. Often, quickness and timing can help counter size. When rebounding, continue to move into position when the defender is following the flight of the ball.

3. In defending the tall opponent, try to "push" him/her away from the basket or spot he/she wishes to maintain. This can be accomplished by getting to the spot first and forcing the opponent to start farther away. Also, if he/she is slow, play up tight and close at all times.

4. When the taller, bigger opponent is defending you, use the drive and cutting to force the slower (probably) opponent to respect your quickness. This will give you more room to work. Always keep moving. Make the slower, bigger player work hard to keep up with you.

When the opponent is smaller and perhaps quicker, consider these strategies:

1. Take the smaller player into the pivot position and "post-up." This will allow you to take advantage of your size and strength.
2. When defending the smaller, quicker opponent, give him/her lots of room so he/she cannot drive and penetrate the basket. Anticipate his/her first move, and try to take it away or force the quicker player to do something that he/she doesn't prefer to do.
3. If the quicker opponent doesn't have the ball, don't allow him/her to get it. Play tight, deny passes, or block passing lanes and make it difficult to get the ball. If he/she doesn't have the ball, his/her quickness advantage is not as powerful.

If the opponent's attitude can be seen as a weakness, try to capitalize on this trait.

1. If an opponent doesn't like pressure, play tight on defense and deny him/her the ball. This often frustrates players into mistakes and errors that will lead to turnovers.
2. If an opponent is having a bad game, don't give him/her anything easy to allow him/her a chance to regain confidence. Make him/her work hard on both ends of the court.

If the opponent is having a great game and clearly has a lot of confidence, try taking away the shots or situations that he/she prefers.

1. If he/she is having a hot shooting night, try to force him/her farther from the basket.
2. Try to deny him/her the ball so he/she cannot shoot.
3. Try to double-team this player whenever he/she receives the ball.

In all cases, look for weaknesses in the opponent. A few examples are:

1. If a player wants to drive only toward one side of the court or dribble with one hand, force him/her to go the other way or use the other hand.
2. If a driver doesn't pass, always defense for a shot. If a driver won't shoot, play for a pass.
3. If a post player turns only one way to shoot, take that side away and make him/her go in the other direction.
4. If you have to foul late in the game to catch up or stop the clock, know who to foul.
5. Use head fakes to get by a "jumper."
6. If an opponent is in foul trouble, take him/her inside and force the action to attempt to get another foul charged to this player.

Glossary

abductors muscles that move away from axis or trunk

acetabulum cup-shaped socket in hip bone

adductor muscles that draw a part toward the median line of the body or toward the axis of an extremity

aerobic training or endurance ability of the cardiovascular system to function efficiently at a high rate for an extended time using oxygen as the main source of energy

agility ability to change or alter, quickly and accurately, the direction of body movement

American Athletic Union (AAU) an organization established to regulate and supervise college athletics

anaerobic training or endurance short duration, explosive activities for which more oxygen is required than is being supplied

anxiety a negatively charged emotional state characterized by internal discomfort and a feeling of nervousness

arousal the intensity of behavior on a continuum from sleep to extensive excitement

baby hook or jump hook a shot taken with one hand in a sweeping motion over the top of a tall defender

back door a cut along the baseline when a player is being overplayed by the defense or when the defense turns to look at the ball

ballistic stretching repetitive, bouncing movements used to stretch a specific muscle

ball your opponent a defensive principle in which the player positions himself/herself between the ball and the offensive opponents

baseball pass a long down-court pass thrown with an overhand throwing motion

baseline the end line running under the basket from sideline to sideline

basket the goal

behind-the-back dribble a dribble behind the back that the main ball handler uses during team offensive play when a defensive player is overplaying the direction of the dribbler

blocking positioning of a defensive player in a manner so as to prevent an offensive player from establishing court position

blocking off the positioning of a defensive player in such a manner as to prevent an offensive player from going to the basket for a rebound

body balance the ability to move quickly in any direction and stop fast with good balance

bounce pass a pass that strikes the floor once before it reaches the receiver

breath control a relaxation technique that involves proper breathing to control anxiety and muscle tension

cardiovascular endurance ability to perform physical activities for extended periods using the heart, lung, and vascular system

center a position usually played by the tallest player on the team, in charge of rebounding, shot blocking, and inside scoring

charging running into a player who is stationary or has an established position

chest pass a two-handed pass pushed from the front of the passer's chest toward the receiver's chest on a horizontal plane

circuit training a series of exercise stations for strength training, flexibility, and endurance

concentration the ability to keep focused on relevant environment cues

Continental Basketball Association (CBA) an organization that provides training and minor league experience

controlled dribble a low dribble close to the body that is used when defensive players are near and the ball must be protected

cross-over dribble a dribble in which the ball is quickly switched from one hand to the other as the ball passes in front of the body

cutter an offensive player who uses a quick movement to elude an opponent so he/she can receive a pass from a teammate while going to an open area on the court or when going toward the basket

cutting making quick moves to get into scoring position when an offensive player does not have the ball

defense the team without the ball, whose objective is to keep the opponent from scoring

defensive rebounding rebounding the ball at the opponent's end of the court when your team is the defensive team; the act of gaining possession of the ball by the defensive team after the offensive team has attempted and missed a field goal

double screen a screen set by two players

double team a defensive tactic of using two players to guard the player who has the ball

dribbling bouncing the ball in a way to advance the ball downcourt, to initiate play patterns, to make drives toward the basket, and to move into good shooting positions

drop step a defensive step that allows the defender to regain or maintain good positioning by doing reverse pivot with back foot and stepping back with lead foot

faking the ability to make an opponent commit himself/herself by making him/her think that the opposing player is going to do something different.

Fartlek training a technique involving running on varied terrain at varying speeds

fast break a situation in which the defensive team gains possession of the ball and moves quickly into scoring position so team members outnumber opponents; the idea is to attempt to score before the opponent's defense can be set up

Federation Internationale de Basketball (FIBA) organization that establishes internal rules for basketball events such as the Olympics

field goal a score that is valued at 2 or 3 points, depending on the distance from where the ball is launched, and is awarded to a player who shoots the ball over the rim and through the net

flagrant foul a foul intended to harm the opponent

flexibility ability to move freely through a full, non-restricted, painfree range of motion

flip pass a pass made with one hand when exchanging the ball at close range

forward an offensive player who is stationed in the forecourt near the sideline toward the corner

foul an infraction of the rules, usually because of contact between opposing players, for which one or more free throws are awarded or ball possession is lost

free throw an unhindered try for a goal from behind the free throw line awarded as a result of a foul by an opponent and valued at one point if scored; also called *foul shot*

free throw shot an unguarded shot from the free-throw line that results from a foul by an opponent

give-and-go passing the ball to a teammate and cutting hard to the basket for a return pass

gluteal related to gluteus muscles, the large muscles of the buttocks

guard an offensive position located away from the basket toward the center line

hamstring one of the tendons at the back of the knee

high post an offensive player who plays near the free throw line

imagery creating or re-creating an experience in the mind

jump ball the situation resolving joint possession, in which the official tosses the ball into the air and two opposing players jump in an effort to tap the ball toward a teammate

jump shot a shot similar in action to one-handed set shot but performed while shooter is in the air

lay-up a shot taken near the basket usually by playing the ball off the backboard; also called *lay-in*

lay-up shot a shot taken close to the basket, usually with one hand

lob pass a pass with a high arc

loose ball a situation in which neither team has possession of the ball

low post an offensive player who plays near the basket with his or her back to the basket

man-to-man a team defense in which each defensive player is assigned to guard a specific opponent

man-to-man defense a team defense in which each defensive player is assigned to guard a specific opponent

man-to-man press similar to the man-to-man defense, in which each defensive player puts pressure on an assigned opponent

muscular endurance ability of a muscle or muscle group to repeat a movement again and again for an extended time

muscular strength ability of a muscle or muscle group to exert maximum force one time

National Basketball Association (NBA) men's professional basketball organization

National Basketball League the first professional league of basketball players organized in 1898

National Basketball League (NBL) a professional basketball league for women

National Collegiate Athletic Association (NCAA) established in 1910 as the new name for the American Athletic Union organized to regulate and supervise college athletics

National Federation of State High Schools Association governing organization that establishes rules for high school basketball play

offense the team that has possession of the ball; also refers to the method a team uses to score baskets, as well as a team's scoring ability

offensive rebounding rebounding the ball at the offensive end of the floor when your team is the offensive team; the act of gaining possession of the ball by the offensive team after a missed field goal attempt by the rebounder or a teammate

one-handed push pass a pass made with one hand, initiated from the side of the body, about shoulder height

out of bounds the area outside of the boundary lines

passing game a type of offense in which players seem to move in a freelance manner, but follow a set of rules

pectoral chest area

perimeter player a player stationed around the outer boundaries of the lane who feeds and shoots the ball

peripheral vision ability to see to the side while looking ahead

personal foul a foul caused by contact with an opponent while the ball is alive

pick and roll an offensive technique in which a player screens for a teammate who has the ball, and then rolls or moves to the basket for a pass

pivot an offensive player position sometimes referred to as a *post*; usually, tall, strong rebounders who can pass and set screens play this position

pivoting a maneuver of the feet to change the direction of the body while one foot keeps contact with the floor

plyometrics jumping from an elevated surface (box) onto the floor and then rebounding (jumping) back into the air as high as possible

point guard an offensive player who is the main ball handler and passes the ball to team scorers

post player a pivot player stationed near the basket and facing away from it

power forward an offensive player who is an aggressive rebounder and usually scores from pick and rolls or offensive rebounds

press a team defense that may be either man-to-man or zone at any point on the floor

pressing defense a forcing type of defense in which the offense is picked up farther away from the basket than normal; press may be half-court, three-quarter court, or full court

press offense a type of offense in which positioning can vary from mid-court, to three-quarter, to full court

principle of individuality each individual's unique response to different activities

principle of maintenance retaining the present level of fitness once the desired level is reached

principle of overload doing more than normal to improve fitness

principle of progression a gradual increase in the amount of exercise done over a period of time

principle of specificity specific kinds of activity to build specific components of physical fitness

progressive relaxation a relaxation technique that involves tensing and relaxing specific muscles sequentially

quadriceps the great extensor muscle at front of thigh

rebounding see defensive rebounding and offensive rebounding

scouting obtaining information about an opponent before playing a game

screen a maneuver the offense uses in an effort to free a player for a shot at the basket; the screener stands in such a position that the opposing defensive player cannot get to the player who is in position to shoot

screening (or pick) a maneuver used by an offensive player who, without causing contact, delays or prevents an opponent from reaching a desired position

secondary break second options for scoring during a fast break if primary options are stopped; usually the trailer is the player designated for these "second options"

shooting guard an offensive player who usually is the best shooter on the team

shuffle offense a continuity offense that requires each player to play all positions

single-post offense an offensive formation in which one player is stationed at either high or low post

slide step a defensive step that allows quick changes of direction by moving the feet into a parallel stance with both feet in line with the direction the player is going

slide-through a defensive technique in which the defensive player glides through the screen and continues guarding the same offensive player

small forward an offensive player who usually is a good shooter and ball handler from the perimeter

speed dribble a dribble in which the body is upright and the ball is pushed out in front to advance the ball quickly downcourt

spinal rotation rotary movement of spine in horizontal plane

split-the-post a three-player offensive maneuver in which the ball is passed to a post player and two players than scissor-off this post player for a possible pass

split vision look one way, pass the other way

spots offense the five major spots on the court that are filled all the time during operation or offense

static stretching stretching a muscle slowly and passively, then holding it in position for an extended time

step-out a defensive technique in which the player defending the screener helps teammates by moving out into the path of the ball handler

stride stop a stop in which the rear foot hits the floor first and becomes the pivot foot with the other foot following

strong-side play play on the side of the court where the ball is currently located

substitutions players who enter the game to match up or counter opponents

switching picking up any offensive player other than the one the defensive player is normally guarding

technical foul a foul by either a player or a nonplayer that does not involve contact or that may involve unsportsmanlike acts with an opponent or official

telegraph to let others know your intentions

tensor fasciae latae small muscle at the front and side of the hip

three-on-two situation one in which three offensive players have an advantage over two defenders during a fast break

time-out a designated period of time a coach or players can take to make changes in game strategy, derail opponents, correct mistakes, and prepare players

tipping a quick, one-handed flip of a missed field goal try that results in a score

trailer an offensive player who comes downcourt after his or her teammates have tried to score on a three-on-two situation; trailer can be available for an outlet pass for a quick shot or to cut through for a lay-up or rebound; fourth player in the fast break who "trails" the primary break and becomes important if the three fillers don't score.

transition skills skills that allow one team to rapidly change from offense to defense and vice versa.

trapping (double-teaming) a defensive maneuver in which two defenders confine an offensive player with the ball and attempt to prevent successful completion of a pass by blocking passing lanes and take away driving or shooting opportunities for the offense

traveling taking more than one step with the ball without dribbling

triple-threat position holding the ball near the hip so the player can pass, shoot, or drive

turnover any loss of ball possession through error or a violation of the rules

two-foot jump stop a stop used when defense is pressuring and an immediate pivot or turn is needed; also used to prepare for a lay-up or jump shot

two-handed overhead pass a pass made with two hands, initiated high over the head

two-on-one situation one in which two offensive players have an advantage over the one defender during a fast break

"V" cut an offensive action that takes the defense in the direction it is playing and then cutting opposite the ball or shot

violation an infringement of the rules in sports that is less serious than a foul and usually involves technicalities of play resulting in loss of possession of the ball

weak-side play play on the side of the court away from the ball

Women's National Basketball Association (WNBA) a professional basketball league for women run by the NBA

zone a team defense in which each player is responsible for an assigned area of the court rather than a specific opponent

zone defense a defensive system in which each player is responsible for an assigned area of the court

zone press similar to zone defense, in which defensive players are assigned to cover an area of the court and anyone in that area

Index